Contents

Introduction

To teacher and pupils

The plays in this book are meant, first and foremost, to be read, acted out and enjoyed in class. They have plenty of parts for everyone. They can also be performed – to other classes (even in assembly if it is long enough), parents and friends. These performances can still be done with a minimum of properties, costumes and scenery. It depends on your school, the resources and the time you have available.

Although the plays are about different subjects and in different styles they all have two things in common.

Firstly, they have been written by playwrights who know what children – and their teachers – want. David Wood is well-known as a writer, director and actor of plays for young people. Andrew Davies has written novels and television plays for children. Steve Eales is a new writer whose plays have been developed from working closely with children as a teacher.

Secondly, all the plays offer opportunities for you to add your own ideas. There is room for extra characters, extra scenes and, in some cases, deliberate gaps for you to try out different ways of 'telling the story'. In the plays themselves and at the end there are suggestions for additional activities or further plays which you might like to do for yourselves.

We have already had fun writing these plays and watching children perform them. We hope you enjoy them as much. Oh, and I think that every play has at least one good part that the teacher could take!

John Alcock
University of Warwick
July 1986

Hoff the Cat Dealer
Andrew Davies

a play with possibilities and gaps

Hoff the Cat Dealer is a play with possibilities: at intervals in the play there are gaps for you to use your own imagination, and the ending is left open so that you can make the play your own. Probably the best way to tackle the play is to read it through as it stands, as a group or a class, noting the possibilities as you go along; then go back and look at the gaps again.

Characters

HOFF the Cat Dealer
MRS HOFF
CAT (PROWLER)
CAT ONE
CAT TWO
CAT THREE
CAT FOUR
CAT FIVE
CAT SIX
CAT SEVEN
CAT EIGHT
CAT NINE
GINGER TOM
CUSTOMER
OTHER CUSTOMERS

SCENE ONE

The Hoff kitchen. MRS HOFF *alone. She speaks to the audience.*

MRS HOFF. No good staring in through my kitchen window. Hoff's
    not back from work yet. Anyway you wouldn't want to know us. We're
    just ordinary.
    We're as ordinary as you.
    If you want to know what we do,
    Hoff works at the car works.
    A bit of a car comes along to Hoff
    And Hoff screws in four screws:
    Not the sort of work you'd choose
    But it pays for the children's shoes.
    And I clean people's houses,
    Do the jobs they don't like to do.
    Too often I've seen my reflected face
    Staring up from the bottom of a rich man's loo.
    I want my turn. I want a good time.
    I want to be rich. Is that a crime?

HOFF (*off*). I'm back!

MRS HOFF. He's early.

HOFF (*coming in*). I've got bad news and I've got good news.

MRS HOFF. What's the bad news?

HOFF. She always likes the bad news first. I've lost my job.

MRS HOFF. Don't cars need screws any more?

HOFF. Yes they do, but they're getting a robot in. It's faster than me
    and they don't need to pay it. OK, Hoff. Push off. So I did.

MRS HOFF. But what are we going to do?

HOFF. Don't you want to hear the good news?

MRS HOFF. What good news?

HOFF. She's always suspicious of good news. We've got a cat.

MRS HOFF. You call that good news? We're starving, and Hoff gets a cat!

HOFF. Wait till you see him. He's almost human. He followed me all the way home. Come in, boy.

CAT (*coming in*). Haywow.

HOFF. Haywow. Say haywow to the cat. He's saying haywow to you.

MRS HOFF (*sarcastically*). *Haywow?*

CAT. Haywow.

HOFF. Would you like some milk, cat?

CAT. Now?

HOFF. Yes.

CAT. Wow!

HOFF. You see? How could anyone be depressed with a cat like this?

CAT. Cherooot?

HOFF. No thanks, I don't smoke.

MRS HOFF. I can't stand this. Hoff, you are going crackers. We cannot afford a cat. You'll have to get rid of him!

She storms off.

HOFF. Wow.

CAT. Meck. Meck.

HOFF. Meck meck? What does that mean?

CAT. Well, not very much, really. Just yes indeed, see what you mean, mate.

HOFF. You can talk!

CAT. Naturally. If you're kind enough to invite me in, give me milk, and talk my language, it's only polite to talk yours as well.

HOFF. Meck. Meck. Wow. Look, I'm not dreaming, am I?

CAT. No.

HOFF. The wife's got a point, you know. You're a splendid cat – what's your name, by the way?

CAT. Prowler.

HOFF. You're a splendid cat, Prowler, but we're absolutely broke. We can't afford you.

PROWLER. Meck. Meck. I see what you mean.

MRS HOFF (coming back). Is that cat still here?

PROWLER. Rubber rubber rubber.

MRS HOFF. He's purring! He thinks he's on to a good thing here!

PROWLER. Madam, if you don't want me, I'll go at once.

MRS HOFF. Hoff! He's talking!

HOFF. Meck. Meck. I know.

MRS HOFF. Perhaps I've been too hasty. A talking cat. We could make money out of that. We could . . . we could get him into television!

PROWLER. Fizz. Fizzzzz.

HOFF. I don't think he likes the sound of that.

PROWLER. I only speak to people I particularly like. But listen. I have a proposition to make. I will give you a choice. You can have me to stay with you, and be your friend for life. Or I'll make you rich. You can choose.

HOFF. But, Prowler, can't we have both?

PROWLER. No. You can't. That's the snag.

MRS HOFF. Oh no it's not. I know what I'd choose!

HOFF. Can we have a minute to talk it over.

PROWLER. Meck meck. Of course. But choose with care.

MR and MRS HOFF get into a huddle.

THE HOFFS. Mutter mutter mutter mutter,
MUTTER mutter mutter mutter . . .

This goes on as PROWLER addresses the audience.

PROWLER. It's an interesting fact of life
For cats, and people too,
If you set your heart on something
You will find your wish come true.
But choose with care, but choose with care:
You don't get your second choice too.
Have you made your minds up?

HOFF. Yes.

MRS HOFF. We want to be rich.
I'm sick of scrubbing people's floors
With curlers in my hair.

HOFF. I –

MRS HOFF. What my husband wants to be
Is a catless millionaire.

PROWLER. Meck. Meck. You will be a millionaire, Hoff, but you won't
be catless. You will be the greatest cat dealer in the world.

MRS HOFF. *A cat dealer?*

PROWLER. A cat dealer, and a cat trainer.

HOFF. But no one can train cats. Cats please themselves.

PROWLER. I can teach you how to have power over cats.
You must learn to be hard.
To buy cats cheap and sell them dear
You must see cats come and see cats go
And never shed a tear.
At the name of Hoff the Dealer
All cats will shake with fear.

HOFF. I don't know that I like the sound of that.

PROWLER. You'll get used to it. Now, first, you have to understand
cat talk. Open your window and listen to the cats of the town.

HOFF *opens the window.*

PROWLER. There.

CAT ONE. Cheroot? Cheroot?

CAT TWO. Parrot. Parrot.

CAT ONE. Haywow.

CAT TWO. Haywow. Cheroot?

CAT ONE. Meck. Meck.

PROWLER. Those are two playful cats meeting for a game in the bushes.

HOFF. Yes, I see.

MRS HOFF. Ridiculous.

CAT THREE. Marie? Marie? Marie?

PROWLER. A small shy cat who doesn't want any trouble.

CAT FOUR. Herrrman the Gerrrman.
    Herrrman the Gerrrman.

CAT FIVE. Rubber rubber rubber rubber,
    Rubber rubber rubber rubber.

HOFF. Wait a minute. Don't tell me. Two fat happy cats who've just had their supper.

PROWLER. Excellent.

MRS HOFF. Rubbish.

CAT SIX. Manyana! Manyana!
    Howard! Howard! Howaaaard!

CAT SEVEN. Manyana! Manyana!
    Zoe! Zoe! Zoeeee!

CAT SIX. Howaaaard!

MRS HOFF. Noisy beasts! Get away from my garden!

CAT SIX. Manyana! Brown banana!

MRS HOFF. Stop that at once!

PROWLER. That's a love song.

HOFF. Yes, I see. Meck meck. I never knew all those cat sounds meant anything.

CAT EIGHT. Wacka-wacka! Wacka-wacka!

PROWLER. A dangerous cat, bold and bad, looking for a fight.

CAT EIGHT. Wacka wacka fizzz. Fizzz. Fizzersplatt!

CAT NINE. Fizz! Fizzz! Fizzzersplattt!

CAT EIGHT. Fizzersplat!

CAT NINE. Fizzfizz . . . ow! Wow, wow, wow . . . (*Fading.*)

HOFF. And he's won!

PROWLER. Very good, Hoff. You're learning fast. But there's a lot more. Study with me carefully all night, and by dawn you'll know cat talk.

MRS HOFF. Ridiculous. I'm going to bed.

PROWLER. Now. Listen again.

What follows is a sort of cat symphony, which you make up yourselves. For suggestions on how to do this, see the notes at the end of the play.

SCENE TWO

Morning

MRS HOFF. Well, that was terrible. I didn't get a wink of sleep all night.

HOFF. It was all in a good cause, dear. A great cat dealer has to know his subject. I really feel I know all about cats now.

PROWLER. Except the most important thing. The thing that will make you a millionaire. How to have power over cats. How to make them do anything.

MRS HOFF. Pay attention, Hoff.

HOFF. I'm listening.

PROWLER. You have to know the cat charm. Come close. Let me whisper. Very, very softly, in a sing-song voice, you have to say:

Miami Yokohama, Miami Yokohama,
Yamana yamana yamana,
Pretzel pretzel pretzel!

MRS HOFF. Is that all?

PROWLER. Believe me, lady, it's plenty. Say it too loud, you'd have
so many cats through that window you'd think your flat was made
of fur. Try it, Hoff. But *quietly*.

HOFF. I feel silly.

MRS HOFF. Oh, go on, Hoff, if it's going to make us rich.

HOFF. All right. Um . . .
Miami Yokohama, Miami Yokohama,
Yamana yamana yamana,
Pretzel pretzel pretzel!

*Cats begin to flop through the window, in ones and twos, then several at
a time.*

CATS. Miaow. Prow. Perrot. Marie!

*More and more cats come in, using any of the cries from the cat
symphony.*

HOFF. There are too many! I can't cope! Stop!

Dead silence. All cats motionless.

PROWLER. You see. They are now under the fantastic power of your
iron will.

HOFF. I don't believe you.

PROWLER. Try one.

HOFF. Let's see. You. Ginger Tom. Um . . . bark like a dog.

GINGER TOM. Row! Row!

HOFF. Amazing. Thank you, Tom.

GINGER TOM (*purring*). Rubber rubber rubber rubber.

MRS HOFF. This is all very well, but I don't see what good it's going
to do. This isn't making us rich.

PROWLER. Mrs Hoff, you still don't understand. These cats will do anything

MRS HOFF. Me? I'd feel a fool, talking to a bunch of cats.

HOFF. Well, you're the one who wants to be rich.

MRS HOFF. We both do, Hoff. We decided. All right then. Look here, you cats.

CATS. Cheroot?

MRS HOFF. You'll have to talk English with me. What can you do to make us rich?

CATS. Anything.

CAT ONE. You can train us to clean houses.

CAT TWO. And we'll capture all the mouses.

CAT ONE. Mice!

CAT THREE. We can go and fetch the papers in the snow and ice.

CAT FOUR. Play the fiddle, sing and dance.

CAT FIVE. Manufacture underpants.

CAT SIX. We can sweep up fallen leaves.

CAT SEVEN. We'll be watchcats! Capture thieves!

CAT EIGHT. We can curl up on your heads like expensive Russian hats!

CAT NINE. Nothing is impossible for Hoff the Dealer's Cats!

CATS. Cheroot! Cheroot! Rubber rubber rubber rubber.

MRS HOFF. Ah, now I see. And when Hoff has trained them, we can sell them for vast sums of money.

PROWLER. Exactly, Mrs Hoff. But first, you have to do your first deal.

HOFF. Why? How? I haven't trained any yet.

PROWLER. First you have to sell me to buy cat food.

HOFF. Sell you? I thought you were going to stay and help me.

PROWLER. You know all you need to know now.

HOFF. But . . . we'll miss you.

MRS HOFF. We'll get over it.

PROWLER. You made your choice, Hoff. You could have had me as a friend for life. But you wanted to be rich.

HOFF. Couldn't we just be *fairly* rich, and be *fairly* friendly for life?

PROWLER. Those are not the terms of the deal!

HOFF. Oh, this is awful. You see the thing is, I'm completely broke . . . if I'd only had a job . . .

MRS HOFF. Hoff, you're pathetic, standing there making excuses to a cat. Come on, let's get him down to the market.

The Market. They stand under a sign:
"Hoff the Cat Dealer".

MRS HOFF. Well, this is a bit of a dead loss.

HOFF (*hopefully*). Maybe no one's going to come. Then we can take him home again.

PROWLER. Oh, no. There's always someone who needs a cat. Look. Here's someone coming.

HOFF. He doesn't look very nice.

PROWLER. You can't choose nice customers. Dealers have to be hard.

MRS HOFF. Of course they have to be. (*Shouts:*) Hoff the cat dealer! Come and get your cats here! Good morning, sir, this is your lucky day.

CUSTOMER. I doubt it. Cat dealer, eh? Let's see your cats.

HOFF. Well, we've only got this one . . .

MRS HOFF. What sort of cat do you need?

CUSTOMER. I want a cat of all work. A mouser. A garden terror. I've got birds eating my blackcurrants, I've got rats in my cellar. I want a twenty-four hour cat, always on the job.

MRS HOFF. Then this is the cat for you. He's got certificates. He's tackled rats the size of corgis. Complete satisfaction or your money back. We're always here.

CUSTOMER. He looks a handy sort of cat.

HOFF. He's a wonderful cat. He can talk. Prowler!

CUSTOMER. You must be barmy.

PROWLER. Miaow.

CUSTOMER. Call that talking?

HOFF. If you're nice to him, he'll be nice to you.

CUSTOMER. I don't buy a cat to be nice to him.

HOFF. Will you feed him well?

CUSTOMER. He can eat the rats he catches. How much?

MRS HOFF. Twenty pounds.

CUSTOMER. Satisfaction or me money back?

MRS HOFF. We're always here.

CUSTOMER. I'll give you five.

MRS HOFF. Done.

CUSTOMER. Right, Moggy. Into the sack with you.

PROWLER. Manyana!

HOFF. Look, wait a minute . . .

CUSTOMER. Good day to you.

PROWLER (*faintly from the sack as he is carried off*). Manyana! Manyana! Manyana . . .

HOFF. Oh, I do feel bad about this. I feel as if I've sold a friend.

MRS HOFF. Hoff, you are soft in the head. Five pounds! And we can turn it into millions! Come on, let's get to work!

Back home.

MRS HOFF. Go on then, Hoff.

HOFF. I'm not in the mood.

MRS HOFF. Dealers are always in the mood.

HOFF. All right then. Here goes.
Miami Yokohama,
Miami Yokohama,
Yamana yamana yamana,
Pretzel pretzel pretzel!

The cats start coming as before.

CATS. Miaow.
Prow.
Perrot.
Marie.

And so on, as many as you like.

HOFF. Stop!

CATS. Rubber rubber rubber rubber . . .

HOFF. Silence, cats.

They are silent.

MRS HOFF. Now. What shall we start with? I know. I'll train the housework cats and you train the watchcats.

And the training begins.

And this is where you can take over: work out some of the things that the cats could be trained to do, and the ingenious cat-like ways in which they could do them. You could do this by discussing and then acting out in groups, or by writing short scenes individually or in pairs. (See suggestions at the end.)

To end this sequence:

HOFF. Very good, cats. You've all done very well.

MRS HOFF. And we're going to do very well out of you.

HOFF. S'pose so.

MRS HOFF. What's the matter with you, Hoff?

HOFF. I still miss Prowler.

MRS HOFF. Who cares about Prowler? We can have all the cats we need, and sell them too. What are you under, cats?

CATS. We are under the fantastic power of your iron will.

MRS HOFF. I'll say you are. And now to business!

The Market. HOFF *has a new, bigger sign:*
HOFF THE MAGIC CAT DEALER.

MRS HOFF. Here it is, folks, the magic cat emporium. Cats for all jobs, cats for all seasons. Whatever you want doing, our cats can do it. But don't take my word for it: they'll speak for themselves! Hoff!

HOFF. Tell them, cats!

CAT ONE. We've been trained to clean your houses.

CAT TWO. And we'll capture all your mouses.

CAT ONE. Mice!

MRS HOFF. He'll never learn, that one.

CAT THREE. We can go and fetch the paper in the snow and ice.

CAT FOUR. Play the fiddle, sing and dance.

CAT FIVE. Manufacture underpants.

CAT SIX. We can sweep up fallen leaves.

CAT SEVEN. We'll be watchcats! Capture thieves!

CAT EIGHT. We can curl up on your heads like expensive Russian hats!

CAT NINE. Nothing is impossible for Hoff the Dealer's Cats!

CUSTOMERS. Amazing! Did you hear that? I'm going to get one! I'm going to get half a dozen!

MRS HOFF. Come on, then! Who's first?

One by one, customers come up and say what they need doing. Use your imagination and be as fantastic as you like. As before, this will need to be worked out in groups or pairs.

To end the sequence:

HOFF. Well, there we are. We've sold the lot.

MRS HOFF. And I've got a shopping bag full of notes. Hoff, we're rich.

HOFF. I wonder what Prowler's doing.

Back home.

HOFF. That's more money than I've ever seen in my life.

MRS HOFF. It's nowhere near a million, Hoff.

HOFF. I know, but we could retire on it.

MRS HOFF. Hoff, we're dealers now. We're in business. We need to expand. Export! Advertise!

HOFF. Advertise?

MRS HOFF. Newspapers, magazines, TV! The world must know about Hoff the Dealer's Cats!

For the next sequence you can make up adverts (base them on adverts you know if you like) for the various things that Hoff's cats can do. A series of three advertisements would be about right.

To end the sequence:

MRS HOFF. There you are, Hoff! Advertising pays! We've made enough money to buy a stately home.

Hoff's stately home.

HOFF. It's very nice, Mrs Hoff. But don't you think it's too big?

MRS HOFF. Not at all. There's all the mail order side, and the accountant's department, and the showrooms, and the banqueting hall. The Prime Minister's coming to tea tomorrow.

HOFF. Oh, dear. Oh, dear.

He looks out of the window.

HOFF. Oh, *dear.*

MRS HOFF. What's the matter now, Hoff?

HOFF. Look at that gang of people coming up the drive.

MRS HOFF. Oh, yes! There's Auntie Edna! And Uncle Bill! And all my Australian cousins! All my relations are coming to stay with us!

She rushes off to welcome them.

HOFF. I never liked the wife's family, you know. When we were poor, they never came near us. Now look at 'em. And this house. It's all very fine, but I don't feel as if I belong in it. Mrs Hoff likes it. She takes to it like a duck to water, all this being millionaires.
And business.
I'm bored with business.
I should have listened to Prowler.
What am I going to do?

What is going to happen?

Discuss how you would like the play to end. There are various possibilities:
HOFF *could sneak off on his own to find* PROWLER.
MRS HOFF *could become fed up with her relations and join him.*
THE CATS *(perhaps aided by* PROWLER*) could stage a takeover.*
HOFF *could gradually deal his way back to where he started by buying dear and selling cheap.*
It's up to you.
Work out a scene, or scenes, to end the play.
You might like to finish with PROWLER's *words:*

PROWLER. It's an interesting fact of life
For cats, and people too,
If you set your heart on something
You may find your wish come true.
But choose with care, but choose with care:
You don't get your second choice too.

THE END

FURTHER SUGGESTIONS

There are 8 points in *HOFF THE CAT DEALER* where you can try out your own ideas.

1 Cat Symphony (page 12)
Make a list of the cat sounds used in the early part of the play, and add some more from your own experience. Work out the best way to spell them. Then, in groups or pairs, work out a pattern of cat sounds based on three or four of them. Then put all the sounds together, gradually working up to a crescendo and dying away into silence.

2 The arrival of the cats (page 13)
Use the same cat sounds but in a different order. This time you need to work up to a climax and stop dead when Hoff gives you the word.

3 What cats can do (page 14)
You might like to look at the rhyming couplets spoken by the cats, and add some more of your own to them. Work as individuals, pairs, or groups; but this time a written script will be essential.

4 Training the cats (page 17)
You've already found out some of the odd things that Hoff's cats can be trained to do or be. Here are some more:
Cats as living scarves and blankets.
Decorative cats to drape around your living room.
Vigilante cats to combat vandals.
Army cats for silent commando raids.
Cat wigs for the bald.
Think of some more of your own, choose an idea that appeals to you, and improvise scenes around them. The scenes you make up could be scenes from the training, or scenes of the cats in action doing their tasks.

5 Selling the cats (page 18)

Choose a couple of ideas you have not used in scenes, and work out scenes with customers. Here are some possibilties:

The singing cats demonstrate.
A Dutch auction.
Trying on the cat scarves.
Cats for snobs, cats for punks, cats for skinheads.

6 Cat advertisements (page 19)

How would Hoff advertise his cats . . .
in the Sunday Times Magazine?
in Jackie?
on TV?

Look at some real examples, adapt them to Hoff's cats, script them, and try them out.

7 Mrs Hoff's relations (page 20)

What would Mrs Hoff's awful relations do?
What could Hoff do about it?
How would the cats react?

8 How to end the play

There could be a number of different endings. Discuss the best way to end the play in class, or in groups; work out what scenes you need then try them out in improvisations. Your ending should bring Prowler back somehow, if the story is to 'round off' in a satisfactory way.

FOLLOW UP POSSIBILITY

Hoff the Cat Dealer is of course a fantasy, but it is based on a very familiar theme: would you rather be rich or happy, and can you be both at the same time? You could try looking at this theme in a realistic way:

Take a family like yours. Think about daydreams: what would each member of the family like to do with a vast sum of money? Probably the ideas would conflict. So imagine a big pools win, or finding a treasure worth hundreds of thousands of pounds. How would life change for the family? What about friends at school? Would the family stay together?

Don't Bother the Animals
Steve Eales

Characters

Main parts

MISS TRIPLEY who should, perhaps, be an adult
WESLEY a keen photographer
JENNIVIVE
SAM who has more than his fair share of problems
TRACEY
IMTIAZ who likes his food
HARVINDER
CARL a know-all
MARIA
MICHAEL
KAMALJIT
SIMA

Smaller parts

FAY
ERROL
ANNA
SEAN
PRITY
THOMAS
WAYNE
JAWAID
SHABNAM
DONNA
REBECCA

Farm animals

COCKEREL
BULL
COW
CALF
GOAT
LAMB
PIG
TWO OTHER CATTLE

MISS TRIPLEY. Everyone off now?

ALL (*shouting*). Yes!

MISS. I beg your pardon.

ALL (*politely*). Yes, Miss Tripley.

MICHAEL. Sam's not, Miss. He's still on the coach.

SAM (*entering*). No I'm not. See. I couldn't get my wellies on, Miss.

MISS. Have you got everything?

SAM. Yes, Miss.

MISS. Everyone got their packed lunch?

SAM. Won't be a minute. (*Goes to get packed lunch.*)

MISS. Right. Into your twos. (*They line up.*) And remember: stay together. I don't want anyone wandering off.

WESLEY. Can I get a picture of us before we go, Miss?

MISS. Yes. If you're quick. (SAM *returns.*)

JENNIVIVE: You mustn't wander off. Miss says.

SAM. I know!

MISS. We've come to the farm to learn and enjoy ourselves, so let's do that, shall we? Lead off, Harvinder.

ANNA. Oh, look, Miss!

(*The* COCKEREL *enters and crows.*)

HARVINDER. Isn't it pretty, Miss. All the colours and that.

PRITY. I don't like the skin bit. It's all . . . flappy.

SHABNAM. Ooh, Miss. It's coming over here.

MISS. Now, Shabnam, what did I say? If you don't bother it, it won't both you. You must remember that for all the animals.

(*The* COCKEREL *starts feeding, then leaves.*)

IMTIAZ. When are we having lunch, Miss?

MISS. Imtiaz, you've not long had your breakfast. Now mind how you go along there. We'll walk up the fields first.

FAY. Isn't it muddy, Miss?

SEAN. Watch where you're going, Errol!

SIMA. Miss! Errol's trodden in some . . .

CARL. Mess, she means, Miss. (*Quickly puts his hand over* SIMA's *mouth.*)

MISS. Wipe it on the grass, Errol. And watch where you're going. Michael and Sean! There's no need to run!

JAWAID. What's this, Miss?

TRACEY. Wheat.

CARL. Barley, actually.

MISS. Yes, it is barley. Come round here, everyone. Do you know the difference between wheat and barley?

SAM. Yes, Miss. You don't get Shredded Barley.

MISS. Anyone got a proper answer?

MARIA. Is one green and the other sort of light brown?

MISS. No. This barley's only green because it's not ripe yet. Later on in the summer it'll go a lighter colour. And that's when it's ready for harvesting. What's harvesting?

ERROL. Picking it, Miss.

HARVINDER. Tying it all into bundles.

MISS. Yes. It's all done by huge machines nowadays called . . .

JENNIVIVE. Combine harvesters.

MISS. So how do we know this is barley?

THOMAS. Is it that bit sticking up?

MISS. Yes, it's called the beard. Bearded barley. And what's it used for?

FAY. Eating?

MISS. Not so much eating. A lot of barley goes to make something we drink. Begins with B as well.

CARL. Beer.

MISS. That's right. All the B's. Bearded barley makes beer.

WESLEY. Hold it, Miss. I want to get a picture.

TRACEY. Barley beards are best for bottles of beer.

KAMALJIT. Clever clogs.

MARIA. Bits of barley beards are bad for bottles of beer.

SEAN. Not true!

ERROL. Clever, though.

CARL. Bottles of best beer are brewed from bags of bearded barley.

IMTIAZ. He always has to be best.

MISS. Let's go on, shall we?

JENNIVIVE. Ooh, Miss! What's that smell?

SIMA. It's horrid!

DONNA. I think it's nice.

WESLEY. It's like vinegar.

MISS. It is a bit. Anyone know what it is? (*Looks at* CARL.) Carl?

CARL. Ooh, I can't remember.

MICHAEL (*looks pleased*). He doesn't know.

MISS. Well. It's silage. You pile up loads of grass and then squash it down hard and it makes silage. And you feed the cows with it in winter.

IMTIAZ. Is it nearly lunch-time, Miss?

MISS. Not yet, Imtiaz. We're talking about feeding cows, not children.

ANNA. There are the cows!

MARIA. They're all the same colour.

PRITY. Black and white.

CARL. Friesian cows, aren't they, Miss?

WAYNE. He would know!

MISS. That's right, Carl. They give very good milk.

SIMA. Can we see them being milked, Miss?

MISS. I don't think it's the right time of day. You'd have to come either very early in the morning or late in the afternoon.

REBECCA (*giggling*). Miss!

MISS. Yes?

WESLEY. Sam wants to know how you get the milk out.

SAM. No I don't!

HARVINDER. He says you lift the tail and pump it out! (*They all laugh.*)

MISS. I don't think even Sam's that . . . Well perhaps I'd better explain. What's the bag called under the cow?

TRACEY. Its udder.

MISS. And that's where the milk collects. And on the udder are four teats. The pink pointed bits. If you pull gently on those the milk squirts out.

JENNIVIVE. They use a machine, though, don't they, Miss?

MISS. Yes. That makes it much easier. No need to use your hands these days. While the cow's being milked by a machine at one end, a machine at the other is measuring out just the right amount of food to give it. The computer works it out.

KAMALJIT. Smart!

SAM (*who has wandered off*). Miss! There's an enormous cow over here!

FAY. That's a bull, stupid!

MICHAEL. Bulls don't have udders.

MISS. That's right. He's probably the husband or father of most of the cows you can see.

SEAN. That's not fair. Only one man.

MISS. You only need one, Sean. One bull will mate with lots of cows, so that they can have a calf and keep making milk for the farmer to sell.

IMTIAZ. Is it time yet, Miss? I'm hungry.

MISS. Let's go and see some more animals first, shall we?

ALL. Ooh, yes.

MISS. There are different cattle over there. (*Some run over.*) Remember, don't bother them . . .

WESLEY, MARIA AND TRACEY. And they won't bother you!

JENNIVIVE. That one looks as if its horns are going up its nose.

SAM (*of Highland cattle*). He needs a haircut!

ANNA. Oh, Miss, look at this one.

SHABNAM. It's got a baby. (WESLEY *takes a photo.*)

THOMAS (*looking at the* CALF). You can eat them, can't you?

ERROL. I don't think I would.

MISS. The meat's called veal. Some people won't eat any sort of meat because they think it's wrong to kill animals for food.

HARVINDER. We don't eat beef.

MISS. That's because in your religion cows are very special. People eat meat or don't eat meat for different reasons.

ERROL. I like beef, but I wouldn't eat little beef.

CARL. Veal.

OTHERS. Nor me.

IMTIAZ. I'd eat my lunch, though, if you let me.

MARIA. I'm starving too.

MISS. All right. Let's find the picnic area.

SAM. Miss! Look what that cow's doing.

MISS. Oh yes, that reminds me. If anyone wants to go to the toilet, now is the time to go. But remember to wash your hands!

ALL. Yes, Miss.

(*Some go.*)

JAWAID. What have you got, Mick?

MICHAEL. Ham in my sandwiches, and biscuits, an orange and an apple.

HARVINDER. I've got tomatoes in my sandwiches.

IMTIAZ. I've got two packets of crisps as well as my sandwiches.

CARL. I've got tuna and cucumber in mine.

PRITY. Look at Wayne.

MARIA. He's got a whole packet of biscuits!

JENNIVIVE (*to* WAYNE). You're greedy, you are.

WAYNE. My mum put them in. I don't want them.

REBECCA. What have you got, Sam?

(SAM *is quiet.*)

DONNA. Show us, Sam. (*He doesn't.*)

ANNA. He's not got anything.

SAM. Yes I have!

TRACEY. Open your bag and show us, then. (*Reluctantly, he does.*) Is that all? Sam's only got a little pork pie.

MISS. No he hasn't. Here you are, Sam. Don't forget the rest of the things you gave me to look after.

(SAM *goes over.*)

SAM (*quietly*). I didn't give you anything.

MISS. I know, but I've got plenty and they won't know.

SAM. My mum never had time to do anything else.

MISS. Mums are busy sometimes.

(*A* GOAT *makes its way unnoticed towards the children.*)

IMTIAZ. I could eat crisps till the cows come home.

TRACEY. Miss said that's till about four o'clock this afternoon.

JENNIVIVE. You'd burst by then!

MARIA (*to Carl*). You sure you know what you're eating? I thought tuna was what you played on a piano.

CARL. That's a tune. This is fish.

SIMA. Do goats like sweets?

KAMALJIT. I don't know.

SIMA. They do, you know.

KAMALJIT. How do you know?

SIMA. There's one eating your Mars bar.

KAMALJIT. Aah! (*He jumps up.*) Miss! My Mars bar!

HARVINDER. It's after my tomatoes!

MISS. Prity, go and see if there's a farmhand around. Perhaps they can lock the goat away till we've finished.

CARL. They eat anything, goats.

MICHAEL. I wouldn't eat you, Carl, even if I were a goat.

FARMHAND. Is she being a nuisance?

IMTIAZ. She's eaten Kamaljit's chocolate.

KAMALJIT. Mars bars are my favourite.

FARMHAND. Nosey creatures, goats. Come on. I'll get you something else to make up for it. And this girl can go in her pen till you've finished.

(*They go off.*)

WESLEY. Can we go round the rest of the farm when we've finished? I want to take some more photos.

MISS. All right. Don't go far. And remember the rule.

MARIA. Don't bother the animals!

(*Some go off.*)

MICHAEL. Kamaljit didn't bother the goat. It bothered him!

WESLEY (*runs on*). Miss! Miss! Quick! The pig's out! Its door wasn't shut properly and I went to take a photo and when it saw me it came towards me and I didn't bother it, Miss. Honest!

(*The* PIG *enters.*)

MISS. Oh, dear.

SAM. I'll see to it, Miss.

MISS. No, Sam. We don't want anyone getting hurt. Sima, go and find the farmhand, will you? (*She goes.*)

IMTIAZ. Miss! It's heading for the food.

MISS. Oh, dear. (*She goes to steer it away.*) Shoo! Shoo!

(*The* PIG *turns round quickly and knocks* MISS TRIPLEY *over.*)

FARMHAND (*running in*). Come here, you big lump of pork! Come on. Back to your pen.

(*The* PIG *goes back.*)

FAY. You all right, Miss?

(MISS TRIPLEY *gets up.*)

MISS. Yes. No bones broken.

HARVINDER. Miss, you're very naughty.

REBECCA. You know what you said.

ALL. Don't bother the animals and they won't bother you!

MISS. And I was right!

SHABNAM. Miss, look!

(*Enter* FARMHAND *with* KAMALJIT *carrying a* LAMB.)

FARMHAND. Don't frighten it. It's not very old. Abandoned by its mum, so we've got to feed it by hand.

TRACEY. Can we stroke it?

FARMHAND. Yes. Be gentle. (*They do.*) Is that your coach over there? It looks ready to go.

(MISS TRIPLEY *checks her watch.*)

MISS. I'd no idea. The time's gone so quickly. Get your things everyone!

WESLEY. Smile, Miss.

SIMA. I thought you were only taking photos of the farm.

KAMALJIT. He is. Teachers are animals.

MICHAEL. Yeah. Wild animals.

MISS. And this teacher will get very wild if you don't get on the coach.

(*They move off.*)

SAM. I don't think you're wild, Miss.

(*He starts to go, turns and gives her a bunch of buttercups before dashing off.*)

MISS. Everyone on?

ALL (*shouting from off stage*). Yes, Miss Tripley.

MISS. Right. Move over, Sam. I'm ready for a sit down!

THE END

FURTHER SUGGESTIONS

Firstly, your class may not have enough people in it to take one part each. You may double and treble parts as you wish. You can give several speeches to one character rather than trying to remember to be several different characters!

You may also wish to introduce other animals or another farmhand.

The children in the play could go on other visits – for example, to a zoo, to the seaside or round a factory. Try to remember the particular characters and how they behave and see if you can decide what they would do and say in other places.

Sometimes you may go on visits as a class yourselves. You could then try making a play about your trip when you get back to school. How did *you* behave? What unusual or amusing things happened or did different people say? Above all, what did you *learn* from your visit? Don't forget that the children in this play learned a lot about life on a farm.

Remember that Wesley, in the play, took along his camera. I wonder how his photos turned out. There are other ways of remembering your visit too – a scrap book, painting, drawing and writing about different things that happened.

Robin Hood and Friar Tuck

David Wood and Dave & Toni Arthur

This play aims to be as flexible as possible. It can be performed in any space, with little or no special costume and scenery, and the minimum of props.

The cast can be virtually as large or as small as required. The whole cast is really a *crowd* of actors who *tell* as well as *react to* the story.

There is one song, for which music is provided, but it is not essential that the song be *sung*; it can be simply chanted in rhythm. It can be accompanied by percussion such as drum beats and tambourines.

A broad style of acting should be encouraged, in the manner of open-air strolling players, sharing their tale with the audience. Audience participation – booing, cheering, etc – is not essential, but would enhance the atmosphere.

The full-length musical play ROBIN HOOD is published by Samuel French Ltd.

Characters

All the actors are part of the crowd listening to the storyteller. Led by him/her, they participate in the story, as though dramatising it as action proceeds. The actors who become characters in the story could be 'selected' by the storyteller. Thus humour could be derived from poor casting! For example, the actor chosen to be Friar Tuck could be too thin, and therefore at first reluctant to perform! The crowd also changes the scene and perhaps encourages the audience to participate.

Individual Speaking Roles

MINSTREL who would hopefully play a guitar, or be
    accompanied by a guitarist
STORYTELLER
FRIAR TUCK
ROBIN HOOD
THREE MEMBERS OF THE CROWD 1 line each

MEMBERS OF THE CROWD play outlaws and dogs

STAGING THE PLAY

The minimum of scenery is necessary.

The acting area can be any shape.

The crowd could begin as part of the audience, watching the play, then participating as required. Certain props *are* necessary, but even some of these are optional.

Cushions to fatten Friar Tuck
Four trick glasses of beer on a tray
A table – this could be the prop table
The stream – blue material or ribbons
Robin Hood's bag
A 'venison' pie
Robin Hood's sword
Weapons for the fight – could be 'sword and bucklers', or staffs
Robin Hood's horn
Dog masks
Staffs for outlaws

The CROWD *wait with the audience.*

The MINSTREL *arrives. Cheers.*

MINSTREL (*sings*). There were stories told in the days of old
Of men of might and main;
But the greatest man was a Nottingham Lamb
And Robin was his name.
Robin, Robin,
And he took his name from the bird in the wood,
And they called him Robin Hood.

There's some would make him a fine Lord's son
A belted Earl at least,
But the silver spoon that he used at noon,
He stole from a canting priest.

He begins to take in the whole audience, encouraging them to join in the chorus.

ALL. Robin, Robin,
And he took his name from the bird in the wood,
And they called him Robin Hood.

As the story progresses, the CROWD *mime out the story as required. The* MINSTREL *nods to individual members of the* CROWD, *who 'become' the character mentioned.*

MINSTREL. His mother she came from a castle fine
But a Yeoman's love she found,
And she left her home with her love to roam
Through Sherwood the seasons round.

ALL. Robin, Robin,
And he took his name from the bird in the wood,
And they called him Robin Hood.

MINSTREL. Robin was born on a bracken couch,
Down on the forest floor,
His mother she wept as the baby slept,
For the home she'd see no more.

ALL. Robin, Robin,
And she took his name from the bird in the wood,
And she called him Robin Hood.

MINSTREL. Robin he grew to a fine young man,
Well-skilled with staff and bow,
And far and near he'd hunt the deer,
That through the woods did go.

ALL. Robin, Robin,
And he took his name from the bird in the wood,
And they called him Robin Hood.

MINSTREL. News has reached the Sheriff's ears
And it's whispered door to door
That young Robin Hood, who lives in the wood,
Robs the rich to feed the poor.

ALL. Robin, Robin,
And they took his name from the bird in the wood,
And they called him Robin Hood.

The member of the CROWD *selected to play* ROBIN HOOD *steps forward and sings or speaks.*

ROBIN HOOD. For the hunting of the King's royal deer,
An outlaw I became,
And I made a vow that I ne'er would bow,
And the rich would fear my name.

ALL. Robin, Robin,

ROBIN HOOD. And I took my name from the bird in the wood,
And they call me Robin Hood.
I gathered the finest band of men,
That walked on English ground,
With the grey goose feather and the silken string
No better could be found.

ROBIN HOOD *selects his outlaws from the* CROWD. *They react flattered or embarrassed.*

There was er . . . (*choosing his 'cast'*) fair Maid Marian and Little John,
They came to join the fun,
And Allen and Will in scarlet still
And Much, the miller's son.
They came to the wood from ev'ry shire
And they ate the doe and buck;
And the hungriest man in the outlaw band
Was the jovial Friar Tuck.

ALL. Robin, Robin,
And he took his name from the bird in the wood,
And we called him Robin Hood.

The CROWD *applaud.*
Three members of the CROWD *join the others.*

1ST MEMBER OF CROWD. How come a friar became an outlaw?

2ND MEMBER OF CROWD. Yes. Hardly the job for a holy man.

3RD MEMBER OF CROWD. Maybe he wasn't wholly holy! Get it? Wholly holy!

Laughter.
The STORYTELLER *steps forward.*

STORYTELLER. No! Friar Tuck joined Robin Hood's band because . . . (*he has an idea.*) We'll show you.

He signals for a fanfare. A hunting horn or drum roll. All except FRIAR TUCK *disperse and return to the* CROWD, *as audience.*

STORYTELLER. The story of Robin Hood and Friar Tuck.

Cheers.

Friar Tuck was the fattest of friars.

FRIAR TUCK *puffs himself up. Perhaps the* STORYTELLER *stuffs cushions up his front.*

The merriest of friars.

FRIAR TUCK. Ho, ho, ho!

STORYTELLER. And the holiest of friars.

The FRIAR *prays.*

In fact it is said Friar Tuck was holier than his socks.

The CROWD *groans.*

And strong. He was so strong he could pick up any man and carry him like a babe in his arms.

A tall member of the CROWD *offers himself to be carried –* FRIAR TUCK *looks at the huge man, decides against it, and picks up the smallest member of the* CROWD. *Cheers and laughter.*

He could eat any man under the table.

FRIAR TUCK *takes the small member of the* CROWD *under a table and mimes biting him.*

What are you doing?

FRIAR TUCK. Eating a man under the table.

Laughter.

STORYTELLER. And when it came to drinking . . . he could drink more ale in less time than any man in Nottingham.

Drum roll. Four tankards of beer (trick glasses) are produced. FRIAR TUCK downs all four pints! Cheers from the CROWD after each glass is drunk.

What's more, the drink had no effect on him whatsoever.

FRIAR TUCK *collapses into the arms of two of the CROWD.*

His eating and drinking habits got him expelled from his abbey.

Two members of the CROWD throw FRIAR TUCK down.

CROWD. Out!

STORYTELLER. As a penance he used to carry travellers over a stream where the bridge was broken.

The CROWD create the stream using blue material or ribbons and rippling them.

One morning he was sitting by the stream, deep in meditation –

FRIAR TUCK *snores.*

when he was interrupted by a voice from the opposite bank.

Enter ROBIN HOOD, carrying a bag, which he puts down on the ground.

ROBIN HOOD. Hey! Fatty Friar.

FRIAR TUCK (*waking with a start*). Mm? What?

ROBIN HOOD. Are you the fat friar that ferries?

FRIAR TUCK. For my sins, I am.

ROBIN HOOD. Good. Carry me across, Friar.

FRIAR TUCK. Certainly, my son. If you come over here, I'll carry you across.

ROBIN HOOD. Right. (*He approaches the water.*) Hey! Wait a minute. You take me for a mug? If I come over to you, I'll have to cross the stream and get wet. Not only that, if I come over to your side and then you carry me across, I'll end up back on this side instead of that side.

FRIAR TUCK. Life is full of little problems, my son.

ROBIN HOOD. I want to get to that side, not this side, and I don't want to get wet. You'll have to come and collect me, fatty Friar.

FRIAR TUCK. Cheek. You can stay there.

ROBIN HOOD. Very well. I'll eat my pie instead.

FRIAR TUCK (*interested*). Pie. Did you say pie?

ROBIN HOOD. Venison. I'd offer you some, if you were over this side.

FRIAR TUCK. Venison you say?

ROBIN HOOD. Best venison pie, yes.

FRIAR TUCK (*tempted*). I'm coming over.

The CROWD *make splish-splash noises as* FRIAR TUCK *wades over the stream. He 'oohs' and 'aahs' in the cold water. He arrives.*

ROBIN HOOD. Welcome, fat Friar.

He prepares to jump on FRIAR TUCK'*s back.*

FRIAR TUCK. You mentioned some pie, my son . . .

ROBIN HOOD. Of course. You can have half of it. Over there.

FRIAR TUCK. Where?

ROBIN HOOD. There.

The 'Over there. Where? Over there,' *becomes a catch phrase, taken up and joined in by the* CROWD *whenever it crops up in the story.*

FRIAR TUCK. Where?

ALL. There!

ROBIN HOOD. Carry me across the stream and I'll give it to you.

FRIAR TUCK (*greed winning the day*). Amen, my son, you win.

The CROWD *make splish-splash noises as* FRIAR TUCK *carries* ROBIN HOOD *over on his back. He puffs and pants under the strain.*

ROBIN HOOD. Thank you, Friar. God be with you.

He starts to go.

FRIAR TUCK. Wait. The, er . . . the pie.

ROBIN HOOD. Of course. I'm sorry.

He feels for his bag.

Oh no. I've left it over there.

He points to his bag on the other bank.

FRIAR TUCK. Where?

ALL. There.

ROBIN HOOD. You'll have to carry me back.

FRIAR TUCK. Oh no, you can get it yourself.

ROBIN HOOD. I'm not really very hungry.

FRIAR TUCK. I am.

ROBIN HOOD. Carry me back, then.

FRIAR TUCK. Amen, my son, you win.

ROBIN HOOD *starts to mount.*

Wait. What happens when I carry you across?

ROBIN HOOD. I give you the pie.

FRIAR TUCK. Then what?

ROBIN HOOD. You carry me back across.

FRIAR TUCK. Oh, no, no. I tell you what. I'll get on your back, you take me back, you give me the pie, you get on my back and I bring you back here.

ROBIN HOOD. Fair enough.

The CROWD *make splish-splash noises as, with difficulty,* ROBIN HOOD *carries* FRIAR TUCK *across.* ROBIN HOOD *finds the pie.*

Thank you, fat Friar, here's your pie.

FRIAR TUCK *starts stuffing his face.*

Come on.

FRIAR TUCK. What?

ROBIN HOOD. You've got to carry me over there.

FRIAR TUCK. Where?

ALL. There.

FRIAR TUCK. Sorry, my son. I never let work interfere with food.

ROBIN HOOD. But you agreed.

FRIAR TUCK. Sorry.

ROBIN HOOD. I'll make you sorry! (*Draws sword.*) I want to cross the stream. Now!

FRIAR TUCK (*reacting to sword*). Amen, my son, you win.

The CROWD *make splish-splash noises as* FRIAR TUCK *carries* ROBIN HOOD *into the 'water'. Then he drops him half-way.* FRIAR TUCK *returns to the bank.* ROBIN HOOD *splashes around in the 'water'.*

FRIAR TUCK (*laughing*). That'll teach you.

ROBIN HOOD *struggles out of the 'water'.*

ROBIN HOOD. You fiendish Friar. I'll teach *you.* Come on. I challenge you.

ROBIN HOOD'*s sword is drawn.* FRIAR TUCK *leaps up eagerly.*

FRIAR TUCK. A fight, a fight. Splendid.

Drum roll. They fight with sword and bucklers. The CROWD *cheers them on.* FRIAR TUCK *is much stronger than* ROBIN HOOD *though. Eventually* ROBIN HOOD *is helpless on the ground.*

ROBIN HOOD. A favour. Grant me a favour!

FRIAR TUCK. Very well.

ROBIN HOOD *blows his horn. Some of the* CROWD *become outlaws, rush in and surround* FRIAR TUCK *and drag him off* ROBIN.

ROBIN HOOD. My men!

FRIAR TUCK. A favour! Grant *me* a favour.

ROBIN HOOD. Very well.

FRIAR TUCK *makes a strange calling noise.*

Other members of the CROWD *put on dog masks and rush on barking. They quickly overpower the* OUTLAWS, *and stand over them, panting.*

FRIAR TUCK. My dogs!

ROBIN HOOD *laughs.*

ROBIN HOOD. A truce! A truce! Good Friar, I like you. You're a man of spirit.

FRIAR TUCK. I like you too. My two favourite activities are food and fighting, and you've given me both. What is your name, my son?

ROBIN HOOD. Men call me Robin Hood.

FRIAR TUCK. You are Robin Hood?

ROBIN HOOD. Yes. And I invite you to become our chaplain and help us further God's work against tyranny and oppression.

OUTLAWS *cheer.*

FRIAR TUCK. I accept.

OUTLAWS *cheer.*

ROBIN HOOD. We shall call you – Friar Tuck! Follow us – the feast is about to start.

FRIAR TUCK. Feast! What are we celebrating?

ROBIN HOOD. I'll give you the toast –

He steps forward formally.

To life in the greenwood,
To flowers and trees,

The sun and the rain,
The birds and the bees,
To justice, to right,
Let us joyfully sing,
To goodness and truth,
To God and our King!

ALL. To God and our King!

Cheers.

FRIAR TUCK. A moment, my son.

FRIAR TUCK *steps forward, and starts his prayer. The others put their hands together solemnly.*

FRIAR TUCK. May the Lord above
Send down a dove
To bring us all his benison
And on my knee
My fervent plea
Is – (*breaking the atmosphere*)
Where d'you keep your venison?

He dashes off, pursued by the laughing, cheering CROWD.

THE END

FURTHER SUGGESTIONS

This play tells how Robin Hood met just one of his Merry Men – Friar Tuck. There are also novels and, above all, ballads, telling how the band of outlaws got together.

You might like to make up for yourselves different ways in which they got together or to turn some of the stories and ballads into plays of your own.

Don't forget that there are opportunities for music and dance in this play. Some members of the class might compose and play instruments or work out the steps of a dance. There are books which tell us about the particular dances they had in the time that Robin Hood is supposed to have lived – and about the kind of food they ate too. You could turn a performance of this play into a party! I am sure that Friar Tuck would approve.

The Thing
Andrew Davies

The Thing takes place in a school, with teachers, pupils, desks, and so on, but the school in this play is, of course, nothing like your school at all. Not a bit of it.

It is intended for reading out loud in class, and as you read it you might like to imagine how you see the Thing.

Characters

LINDA a girl in Class Z
AMRIK a boy in Class Z
NATHAN a boy in Class Z
MISS CUCUMBER form teacher of Class Z
HEADMASTER
MR SPROUT an ill-fated gym teacher
THE THING a Thing
PUPILS
STAFF Lines spoken by pupils or staff should be taken by
    the whole group or class reading the play

LINDA. It seemed like just an ordinary day. Hang up your coats, meet your friends, go to the form room, sit down . . . and there it was! On the very next chair to mine! I can't describe it. It was like . . . well, it was all sort of . . . no, you'd have to see it for yourself. But then Miss Cucumber came in and it all started.

MISS CUCUMBER. Good morning, Class Z.

CLASS. Morning, Miss Cucumber.

LINDA. Miss! There's a thing!

MISS CUCUMBER. First things first, Linda. What's the Class Z motto for registration?

LINDA. Aw, but Miss Cucumber –

MISS CUCUMBER. Quiet!
If we want an orderly day . . .

CLASS (*mournfully chant*). We have to begin in an orderly way.

MISS CUCUMBER. Right. Number off, please.

(PUPILS *call out numbers in the order in which they sit. Try to vary high and low voices, loud and soft voices.*)

PUPIL. One.

PUPIL. Two.

PUPIL. Three.

PUPIL. Four.

PUPIL. Five.

PUPIL. Six.

PUPIL. Seven, Miss.

PUPIL. Eight.

PUPIL. Nine.

PUPIL. Ten.

PUPIL. Eleven.

PUPIL. Twelve.

PUPIL. Thirteen.

PUPIL. Fourteen.

LINDA. Fifteen.

THE THING. Broop.

MISS CUCUMBER. What was that?

THE THING. Broop.

MISS CUCUMBER. David Perkins, stand up. I'm surprised at you.

LINDA. Miss, it's not David Perkins, it's a Thing.

NATHAN. Maybe the Thing is David Perkins. Maybe he's turned into a Thing.

AMRIK. Mayby the Thing has eaten David Perkins.

THE THING. Broop.

AMRIK. He says he has, Miss.

LINDA. No, he doesn't. He says he's not doing any harm, Miss.

MISS CUCUMBER. All right, Class Z, joke over. Now, what have you got to say for yourself, David . . . arrgh! Its a *Thing*!

LINDA. We tried to tell you, Miss.

MISS CUCUMBER. All right. Keep calm. Everybody sit very still. Pay close attention and *don't panic*.

THE THING. Broop broop.

MISS CUCUMBER (*squeals*). Oo! No. I must keep calm. This may be a test of my skill as a teacher. A test devised by Her Majesty's Inspectors, to see whether I measure up or not. A good teacher must be prepared for the unexpected, and now it has come. Perhaps it *is* a school inspector, come in disguise to test me out. Oh, I'm so nervous. Pull yourself together, Marigold.

(*She clears her throat.*)

Ahem. Are you . . . David Perkins.

THE THING. Broop.

NATHAN. He says he is!

AMRIK. He says he's ate him.

THE THING. Broop.

AMRIK. Says he's going to be sick, Miss.

MISS CUCUMBER (*screams*). Quiet! (*Soft voice:*) Quiet. Now, David, if it is David, we've all had a good joke. Just get out of that silly costume, and we won't say any more about it.

THE THING. Broop.

MISS CUCUMBER. Quickly, or you'll be in serious trouble.

THE THING. Broop.

MISS CUCUMBER. Please! (*She's getting pathetic.*)

LINDA. Leave him alone, Miss, he's all right.

MISS CUCUMBER. I shall be the best judge of that, Linda. Now get out of that silly costume or I shall take it off you myself.

CLASS. Ooh! Miss Cucumber!

MISS CUCUMBER. Quiet! Now I'll show you I am not to be trifled with, even though I may be a delicate young woman.

And she advances on THE THING.

MISS CUCUMBER. Now! Come here!

THE THING (*growling*). Broop broop. Brooop!

MISS CUCUMBER (*squealing*). Oo! (*Recovering:*) All right then. Stay as you are. I shall not enter into an undignified struggle. (*To herself:*) It cannot be David Perkins. He would never growl at me like that. It must be an inspector. Inspectors have been known to growl. Oh dear, it is, it must be an inspector, and he has seen me in a panic. (*To* THE THING:) Just my little joke, sir, really. Of course I realised who you were all the time.

THE THING. Broop.

MISS CUCUMBER. I'm very glad you've called in, sir. Would you care to see some of my Projects and Displays? I take a special pride, sir, in the neatness of my noticeboard.

THE THING. Broop. (*Obviously 'no'.*)

MISS CUCUMBER (*disappointed*). Oh. Perhaps a little later?

THE THING. Broop.

MISS CUCUMBER. Then, er . . . may I continue with the register, sir?

THE THING. Broop.

MISS CUCUMBER. Thank you, sir. From seventeen, continue.

PUPIL. Seventeen.

PUPIL. Eighteen.

PUPIL. Nineteen.

Door opens.

PUPIL. Twenty.

Class stands up as HEADMASTER *comes in.*

MISS CUCUMBER. Oh, Mr Marrow . . .

HEADMASTER. Something the matter? Some sort of problem? Has my watch gone wrong? Or am I going mad perhaps? Can Class Z still be in their room when we are already five minutes into period one? Are you all an optical illusion, I ask myself?

MISS CUCUMBER. Mr Marrow –

HEADMASTER. Playing you up, are they? Playing you up? Soon see about that. Life's too short to fool about with. Now, Class Z.

THE THING. Broop.

HEADMASTER. What? Do my ears deceive me?

THE THING. Broop.

HEADMASTER. Aargh! What a shock to the system. Miss Cucumber. Tell me. Am I blind, or mad, or is there a boy in the third row without a school uniform?

MISS CUCUMBER (*urgent whisper*). Not a boy, Mr Marrow. It's a *School Inspector*.

HEADMASTER (*instant change of tone*). Well, of course it is, just my witty way, never a dull moment here, you know, delighted to see you, delighted, always delighted, we have nothing to hide here. (*In a whisper to* MISS CUCUMBER:) Warn the rest of the staff – (*Normal tone again:*) Ha ha ha, just a private jest. Now, perhaps you'd like to come along to my study for a little . . . Miss Cucumber. This is not a school inspector.

LINDA. Please, sir, we know, it's a . . .

HEADMASTER. Quiet, girl. I am using my logical mind here, and logic tells me this is no school inspector. School inspectors do not sit with the children. They loll about in my room drinking my sherry and making sarcastic remarks. They do not say Broop. They say: Marrow, you've been at the petty cash again. No they don't, slip of the tongue, ha ha. They arrive in big cars. Has this thing got a big car?

AMRIK. No, sir.

HEADMASTER. There you are then. Logic! That's what got me where I am today.

AMRIK. Sir, he's eaten David Perkins.

HEADMASTER. Has he now? Do school inspectors eat boys? *Hardly ever*. Logic again. Inspectors wear smart suits. Has it got a smart suit on? No, it has not . . . In fact . . . Miss Cucumber! It seems to have no suit at all! There is a naked Thing in Class Z! Close your eyes, boys and girls, at once. Nakedness is only for Biology and Showers! Class . . . dismiss! I shall deal with this Naked Thing in private!

NATHAN. But we can't see, sir!

HEADMASTER. Feel your way, boy, feel your way! Initiative test! Class Z! Grope your way out! And no giggling!

Class Z grope their way out.

HEADMASTER. Now. Miss Cucumber. Here we are, alone with a Naked Thing.

THE THING. Broop.

HEADMASTER. Quite.

MISS CUCUMBER. Mr Marrow. To you, in private, I can admit it. I'm frightened of this Thing.

HEADMASTER. Have no fear, I shall protect you, my little wilting flower. I am strong and brave, and I have logic on my side. That is why I am Headmaster while you are the lowest of the low, as teachers go. Now, Thing.

THE THING. Broop.

HEADMASTER. See how it responds to the power of my iron will. Now, Thing.

THE THING. Broop.

HEADMASTER. Listen to me. You may be from another world, you may have eaten David Perkins, you may be David Perkins in another form, you may be a figment of my imagination. That is all beside the point. What's important is this. You are in my school and you are not wearing school uniform, and that must be put right at once. Rules are rules.

THE THING. Broop.

HEADMASTER. I am glad you agree. Luckily, I come prepared. (What's luck got to do with it? I am *always* prepared.) Here is a school tie. Here is a school badge. There you are. Wear them with pride, and never let the school down.

THE THING. Broop.

HEADMASTER. Not at all, my dear Thing. I feel proud of you already. Doesn't it look a smart Thing now, Miss Cucumber?

MISS CUCUMBER. It's, er, it's still naked, Mr Marrow.

HEADMASTER. Beside the point, Miss Cucumber. Now, Thing. Pay attention. Miss Cucumber will give you a fiendishly difficult test in Basic Skills, after which you will write out the School Rules and learn them. Understood?

THE THING. Broop.

HEADMASTER. Good. Now for a lie down. I feel quite exhausted. No, don't get up, Thing.

THE THING. Broop.

HEADMASTER. Stay in your seat! I command you!

MISS CUCUMBER (*frightened*). Oh, Mr Marrow!

HEADMASTER. No! I forbid you to leave the room! I shall stand in your way!

MISS CUCUMBER. Oh, be careful, sir!

HEADMASTER (*gritting his teeth*). So you would, would you? (*Changing his tone completely.*) Yes, I see you would. Well, Thing, I've changed my mind. Sign of a great man, ability to change the mind. Why don't you wander round and have a look at the school, relax and enjoy yourself, you can do your tests later. That's the way, my dear chap. Off you go!

(*Door closes.*)

HEADMASTER (*slightly embarrassed*). Changed my mind, Miss Cucumber.

MISS CUCUMBER. You – you tried to stop him and you couldn't.

HEADMASTER. Not at all, Miss Cucumber. I used my Flexibility. Tell them to go the way they want to go. It's a kind of judo of the mind, Miss Cucumber. Nothing to worry about.

MISS CUCUMBER. You couldn't stop him. Who knows what he might be doing now? He might be running wild around the school. Who are we to say he hasn't eaten David Perkins? Or look at it another way. Perhaps he is a troubled soul. Perhaps he needs our help. Perhaps he has Personal Problems. At college they taught me to seek out problem children and care for them, Mr Marrow. Mr Marrow, are we failing this Thing!

HEADMASTER. Miss Cucumber! You forget yourself. Who is Headmaster here, you or me? I saw his problem at once. No school uniform! I gave him a tie and a badge! What is that if not caring for him? Now he can feel Part of the School. I feel sure he won't let us down. He will be a credit to us!

MISS CUCUMBER. Oh, Mr Marrow. I wish I could believe it.

HEADMASTER. It's your job to believe it, Miss Cucumber. Have I not said it? When the Headmaster tells you that everything is all right, everything *is* all right. Even if it isn't. I call that the power of positive thinking. Now, go and teach people things. That's what you're paid for, isn't it?

MISS CUCUMBER. Yes, sir.

HEADMASTER. Of course it is. Run along then, there's a good girl.

LINDA *speaks to the audience.*

LINDA. We didn't see the Thing for quite a bit after that. It seemed just like an ordinary day, except that we knew he was around the school somewhere.

THE THING. Broop broop. Brooop.

LINDA. And it felt sort of nice. Hearing him, and knowing he was there.

NATHAN. Hark at her. I think she fancies him.

LINDA. No I do not! I just like him.

AMRIK. Even if he's eaten Perkins?

LINDA. I like him better than David Perkins. Anyway, he hasn't eaten David Perkins.

NATHAN. How d'you know?

LINDA. He wouldn't eat anyone. I can tell. He's all right if you don't muck him about. Like anyone else is.

NATHAN. She fancies him.

LINDA. Nathan, you are *boring.* It's much more interesting than that. I want to know what he's come to our school for.

AMRIK. Can't be the school dinners.

LINDA. Listen. Can you hear him?

NATHAN. No.

LINDA. Listen again.

A very distant 'Broop. Broop.'

AMRIK. That's him.

LINDA. It sounds as if it's coming from the gym.

In the gym.

MR SPROUT. Right, come on, late boys at the end of the row, cross your legs, sitting, hands outside your knees, hold your toes. What . . . a . . . shower. What a terrible shower. What are you?

CLASS. A terrible shower.

MR SPROUT. What are those?

CLASS. Our bodies, sir.

MR SPROUT. I wouldn't have 'em as a gift. Look at my body. It is strong. It is fit. What is it?

CLASS. Strong and fit, sir.

MR SPROUT. You are quite right. It is. And now I am going to make your bodies strong and fit. Today we will do vaulting. Over the horse. Get in line, shortest at the front, tallest at the back. MOVE! What is this? What is this that meets my eyes?

CLASS. Don't know, sir.

THE THING. Broop.

CLASS. It's a Thing, sir.

MR SPROUT. You are quite right, it is a Thing. It is an 'orrible thing. It is the most 'orrible Thing I 'ave ever 'ad in my gym. Come here, Thing.

THE THING. Broop.

MR SPROUT. I am amazed. I am amazed and 'orrified. Where is your vest, clean white cotton, with name clearly marked?

THE THING. Broop.

MR SPROUT. Where are your shorts?

THE THING. Broop?

MR SPROUT. Where are your dazzling white plimsolls, running about for the use of?

THE THING. Broop.

MR SPROUT. Oh do not plague me with excuses, I 'ave 'eard them all. They are in the wash, bad boys 'ave stolen them, the dog 'as eaten them, you thought it was Tuesday, you 'ave a verruca, you have broken your leg in three places . . . Is that it, eh? Mr Sprout is not impressed, Mr Sprout is not moved to pity. If you 'ave not got a note you will do gym, if you 'ave a note you will shuffle about in the rain and pick up litter. 'Ave you got a note?

THE THING. Broop.

MR SPROUT. Then you will do gym.

THE THING. Broop.

MR SPROUT. I wouldn't have it as a gift. I say I would not give that body to my dog for his dinner. Never mind. I will make you fit and strong. Would you like to be fit and strong like me?

THE THING. Broop.

MR SPROUT. Good. There is the horse. When I say go, I want you to run towards the horse and leap in the air. Are you with me so far?

THE THING. Broop.

MR SPROUT. Leap in the air, perform a double Barani with two and three-quarters twist in the pike position, and land lightly on your horrible dirty toes. Is that clear?

THE THING. Broop.

MR SPROUT. Do not fear. Mr Sprout will stand by the horse and catch you if you stumble.

THE THING. Broop.

MR SPROUT. Right, you horrible thing. On your marks. Get set. Go!

THE CLASS. Cor! Look at him go! Wow!

MR SPROUT. Too high, Thing, too high! Steady!

THE CLASS. He's coming down!

MR SPROUT. Not on me! Help! Aargh. (*Weakly:*) Now look what you have done. You have damaged my world-famous body.

THE THING. Broop.

THE CLASS. He's fainted. He's *dead*!!

Pause.

A bell clangs.

BELL. Clang clang clang.

HEADMASTER. Listen to me, boys and girls. Pay close attention. You may noticed some strange things going on in school today. Do not be alarmed. They are all part of a plan of mine to keep you on your toes.

THE THING. Broop.

HEADMASTER. Everything is under control.

LINDA. What about Mr Sprout?

HEADMASTER. Reports of Mr Sprout's death have been greatly exaggerated. Accidents are bound to happen in the hurly burly of gymnasium life. Mr Sprout is resting. Soon he will be himself again.

MISS CUCUMBER (*anxious whisper*). He's not breathing, Mr Marrow.

HEADMASTER. I didn't say he was breathing, did I? I didn't say he was actually breathing. I said he was not particularly dead. And I am the Headmaster, and what I say goes! Am I right?

THE THING. Broop.

HEADMASTER. Of course I am. Now, boys and girls. Because of the, er, unusual events this morning, I and my staff are going to have an

Emergency Staff Meeting. That does not in any way imply that there is an emergency. Far from it. It's just a turn of phrase.

THE THING. Broop.

HEADMASTER. Quite. And because of the staff meeting, we have granted you an extended lunch hour.

PUPILS. Hooray!

LINDA (*to audience*). Something strange happened during that extended lunch hour. It's hard to explain to anyone who wasn't there. You see, the Thing came out and played with us.

AMRIK. First he played our games.

NATHAN. He was brilliant!

AMRIK. He broke all the rules!

NATHAN. He made you feel the rules didn't count.

LINDA. As if there were new rules.

NATHAN. Yeah.

LINDA. Better than the old rules.

NATHAN. Yeah.

LINDA. And then he taught us his games.

AMRIK. Tree juggling!

NATHAN. Coal polo!

LINDA. Brooping the broop!

AMRIK. And his cap never fell off.

THE THING. Broop broop.

LINDA. It was like he was proud of it.

THE THING (*proudly*). Broop.

LINDA. By the end of that extended lunch time we all felt like making him school captain or something.

THE THING. Broop.

LINDA. And all the time that staff meeting was going on.

HEADMASTER. Serious matter, very serious.

THE STAFF. Rhubarb, rhubarb, mixed greens, very.

HEADMASTER. Take Mr Sprout. He may not be particularly dead at present, but even a slightly dead gym teacher is quite a cause for concern.

THE STAFF. Rhubarb, rhubarb, Guernsey tomatoes.

HEADMASTER. And then there was the matter of the uniform.

THE STAFF. Rhubarb, rhubarb, absolutely radishes.

HEADMASTER. I am glad to find you behind me in this matter.

MISS CUCUMBER. But Mr Marrow!

HEADMASTER. Yes, my dear, speak up, don't be frightened. You may be an insignificant twerp but everyone deserves a hearing.

MISS CUCUMBER. Well, Headmaster, don't you feel we're being a little unfair?

HEADMASTER. Unfair? Unthinkable!

MISS CUCUMBER. The Thing sat in my class, Headmaster. I feel that he – that it – meant well.

HEADMASTER. Meant well? Meant well? Look at poor Sprout there!

THE STAFF. Rhubarb, rhubarb, Sprut's avocado.

HEADMASTER. No turnips about it. We must expel the Thing. It has Let Down the school.

MISS CUCUMBER. But sir! But sir! I feel that we could help the Thing!

HEADMASTER. Miss Cucumber. You seem to be making the elementary mistake that we are here for the benefit of every Tom, Dick, Harry or Thing who chooses to come along and take advantage of us. And we are not! Are we?

THE STAFF. Rhubarb, rhubarb, not on your lettuce.

HEADMASTER. Very well. We are agreed. Call in the Thing.

MISS CUCUMBER. Er . . . Thing, dear. Would you come in now, please?

THE THING (*coming in*). Broop.

HEADMASTER. Now, Thing. My staff and I have considered this matter carefully. Haven't we, ladies and gentlemen?

THE STAFF. Rhubarb, rhubarb.

HEADMASTER. And with the very greatest respect, and our deepest regret, we have decided that the time has come for a parting of the ways. We must prune our pupil-teacher ratio. We have to trim the work force. We find you surplus to present requirements. We don't want to stand in your way. In fact, we're going to let you go. Or in other words, we're going to throw you out. Thing, you're expelled. You can come back and see us on Open Days.

THE THING (*brokenly*). Broop.

MISS CUCUMBER. Headmaster . . . I believe it's crying! I see a tear on its cheek. Goodbye, Thing.

THE THING. Broop.

The THING *goes.*

HEADMASTER. Now, boys and girls. The crisis is over! Work to do, work to do! Needlework, basketball, Ugandan verbs!

LINDA. Broop.

THE THING (*in the distance*). Broop broop.

LINDA (*joyfully*). Broop broop broop!

HEADMASTER. Linda Sydes! How dare you?

NATHAN. Broop.

AMRIK. Broop.

HEADMASTER. Very witty. Now get to your lessons.

PUPILS (*both together and at random*). Broop. Broop broop broop broop.

THE THING (*in the distance*). Broop broop.

PUPILS. Brooop!

HEADMASTER. Where are you going? Come back! I command you!

MISS CUCUMBER. Now see what you've done!

HEADMASTER. Come baaaack! (*Change of mood, as before.*) Right, fine, off you go. We can get along much better without you. Staff, to your lessons.

THE STAFF. Rhubarb, rhubarb, carrots and peas.

HEADMASTER. That's the way.

MISS CUCUMBER. But, Headmaster, there's no one left to teach. There's nothing to do!

HEADMASTER. Miss Cucumber, you're making elementary mistakes again. You're talking as if the school were for the benefit of the pupils, instead of the other way round. That way madness lies, Miss Cucumber. My goodness, is that the time. To work, to work!

THE STAFF. Rhubarb, rhubarb, carrots and peas, rhubarb, rhubarb . . . (*and so on, fading.*)

PUPILS (*in the distance, fading*). Broop. Broop. Broop. Broop. Broop.

THE END

FURTHER SUGGESTIONS

When you have read the play, compare notes on how you imagined the Thing would look. You might like to draw his portrait.

You might also like to discuss the ways in which the school in the play is different from your school.

Some plays have morals, like fables. Do you think that this play has a moral? If so, what is it?

Can you think of any way in which *The Thing* could be performed as a theatre play, for an audience? The only way we can think of is to stage it in the middle of a hall or gym, with the audience round the sides. The Thing would have to be invisible to the audience, though the actors would all have to 'see' it very clearly. This would get over such problems as the Thing falling on Mr Sprout from a great height.

What do you think might happen *after* the end of the play? Could things go on like that? Surely the pupils would have to go back to school? What about the Thing, then? Would the head take him back, or would the Thing go off for further adventures? If so, where would it go, and what sort of adventures might it have?

You might like to write a story or a playscript called *The Thing: Part Two* or *Return of The Thing*.

Handscapes
Steve Eales

Characters

ARTIST written for a girl, but easily adapted for a boy by
  changing 'she' to 'he'
BOY
GIRL
HANDSOME chief handy helper
39 HANDY HELPERS They are numbered and sit in a row
  around the acting area. Parts can be doubled as
  necessary.

HANDY HELPERS 1-13 (*they stand as they speak*).
We have a friend – an artist –
We think you ought to meet.
She's not the sort of person
You would pass by in the street.

HANDY HELPERS 14-26. Some people think her strange.
We thought so, at one time.
She doesn't often talk with words.
She uses paint and mime.

HANDY HELPERS 27-39. We too have learnt her silent talk.
Please watch and learn it too.
Look closely at her paintings.
You may see part of you.

The ARTIST *walks on carring an imaginary easel and paintbox. She puts down the box, sets up the easel, opens the box, puts paper on the easel, takes a brush and paint and begins to work. Along come two children.*

BOY (*pointing*). Hey, look!

GIRL. What's going on?

BOY. Let's find out.

They walk over to the ARTIST *and stand behind her at a distance.*

GIRL (*points at picture and silently mouths*). What is it?

BOY (*shrugs shoulders and then moves forward*). Excuse me.

ARTIST. Oh. Hello.

She shakes hands with him and then with the girl.

BOY. We don't mean to be rude, but . . .

GIRL. What are you painting?

ARTIST (*still working*). Oh, just another handscape.

GIRL. Handscape?

BOY. Don't you mean 'landscape'?

ARTIST. No. I paint hands. Only hands.

GIRL. Don't you get fed up painting the same thing?

ARTIST. Never. No two paintings are the same.

BOY. But if they're all hands . . .

ARTIST. Different hands. In every picture the hands are doing something different. (BOY *and* GIRL *look puzzled.*) Think of your own hands. (*They look at them.*) You can remember when they've been hot (*they nod*) and cold, (*they nod again*) wet and dry. (*They nod.*) They have made things and destroyed things. (*A guilty nod.*) They have been helpful and hurtful. Those hands have probably even killed.

GIRL. Oh, no. That's one thing they've never done.

ARTIST. And yet people swat flies and put worms on their fishing hook

BOY. I suppose you're right.

ARTIST. There are many different things that hands do. Come on. I'll let you meet some friends of mine. I call them my handy helpers. They're always willing to help me show people what hands can do. This is Handsome.

HANDSOME (*steps forward and shakes hands*). How do you do?

ARTIST. He'll get them organised for us.

HANDSOME. Pleasure. If you'd like to settle yourselves down, (*they sit*) we'll do our little party piece. We like this.

The HELPERS *do the actions.*

Handy Helpers, please stand up and give those hands a shake.
Handy Helpers, rub those eyes and make sure you're awake.
Raise your hands above your head and give yourselves a clap.
Then sit down and place both hands back nicely on your lap.
Right. We're all warmed up and ready now.

ARTIST. Good. Do you remember shaking hands with me when you said hello?

BOY AND GIRL. Yes.

ARTIST. Well, you really didn't need to speak at all. The hands were doing the talking for you.

HANDSOME. I bet you can tell what these are saying.

In turn the HANDY HELPERS *mime, freezing until* HANDY HELPER 6 *makes a noise.*

HANDY H1 *finishes eating and holds plate up for more.*

HANDY H2 *looks cross, points at someone and beckons with finger.*

HANDY H3 *mother buttons up coat of child, pats head, waves goodbye.*

HANDY H4 *is bored: scratches face, folds arms, puts hands in pockets. Then sees bus coming and thrusts out arm.*

HANDY H5 *bounces ball, throws it up and catches it, throws it forward: it hits something. Hand goes over mouth.*

HANDY H6 *takes out handkerchief, opens it, blows nose making a loud noise, puts handkerchief away. All sit.*

GIRL. I think the nose spoke more than the hands there.

ARTIST. But it needed the hands.

HANDSOME. Sometimes only the hands will do.

HANDY HELPERS 7 *and 8 mime sitting side by side in a car. 7 gets out and begins to direct 8 into a parking space. There are many attempts, with hands guiding, banging the bonnet, changing gear, steering, waving to say 'no', giving the 'thumbs up'. Finally 8 puts on the brake, turns off the engine and gets out, slamming the door. 8 sits, while 7 scratches head in amazement. Then 7 sits.*

HANDSOME. Come to think of it, hands are very good for showing your feelings.

As before the HANDY HELPERS *mime in turn, freezing until 13 slams the door.*

HANDY H9 *is crying: holding face, wiping eyes.*

HANDY H10 *fingers crossed as if wishing for horse to win a race. Freeze with hands thrown in air as if horse has won.*

HANDY H11 *is worried: rub hands together, clench fists. Freeze with hands clasped over mouth.*

HANDY H12 *strokes dog lovingly, tickles its tummy. Freeze with hands holding dog's head, smiling at it.*

HANDY H13 *is angry: clenches fists, walks up and down, holds sides of head, opens door and slams it. All sit.*

BOY. We need hands for working as well, don't we?

HANDSOME. Writing (14 *stands and writes*), telephoning (15 *telephones*), adding up (16 *counts awkwardly on fingers*) are jobs we all do. (16 *is still struggling to count to ten.*) Of course, some of us use calculators to add up and some of us (16 *reaches ten, sighs and smiles and looks at* HANDSOME) don't. (*The smile disappears and* 16 *sits.*)

HANDSOME. Course, some people's hands have been trained to do special jobs. Can you tell whose hands these are?

GIRL (17 *mimes*). Policewoman, controlling traffic. (17 *sits.*)

BOY (18 *mimes*). Milking a cow. Farmer! (18 *sits.*)

GIRL (19 *mimes*). Drilling . . . putting a screw in . . . doing woodwork!

HANDSOME. That's right. A carpenter. (19 *sits.*)

BOY (20 *mimes*). Pottery. Making a vase or something. (20 *sits.*)

GIRL (21 *mimes*). Somebody washing their hands. What's so special about that?

HANDY H21. To get rid of germs. (*Pulls gloves on tight.* 9 *steps forward.*) Right, ready to begin. Scalpel, nurse. (*They freeze and sit.*)

BOY. A surgeon's hands certainly are important.

HANDSOME. Course, hands aren't only important for working. We need them for playing with too. These people wouldn't be much good without them.

22 steps forward. He taps a music stand with a baton and conducts an orchestra. 23, 24, 25, 26 and 27 are the orchestra, playing double bass, trumpet, harp, violin and cymbals. Sound effects can be made by those miming as each instrument is brought in by the conductor, who then calls a halt.

HANDY H22. I'm sure it'll be all right on the night. (*Sits.*)

GIRL. And sportsmen. They use their hands all the time.

BOY. For swimming. (28 *mimes arms and breathing of breast-stroke.*)

GIRL. Netball. (29 *mimes.*)

BOY. Cricket. (30 *mimes.*)

GIRL. Rowing. (31 *mimes.*)

BOY. Tennis. (32 *mimes.*)

GIRL. Fencing. (33 *mimes.*)

BOY. And entertainers. (*Sports' mimers stop and sit, except for* 31.) A lot of them.

HANDSOME. Come in number 4, your time is up! (31 *returns to place.*)

BOY. A lot of entertainers practise for years to become clever with their hands.

34 steps forward, juggles, bows and sits. 35 steps forward and raises an arm to introduce 36 as the magician. 36 pushes up sleeves to reveal nothing, takes out a handkerchief, holds it out, shows each side, bunches it, and out of the handkerchief a bird appears which is taken away by 35. After bowing, they sit.

ARTIST. Some people have hands which can do things that most of us can't. But don't forget there are some people who cannot do what most of us can. They may need our help. For instance . . . 37 *is a baby.* 38 *puts a bowl of food in front of* 37. 37 *puts hands awkwardly in the bowl and splatters food on the table, throwing it everywhere!*

HANDSOME. Let's try again. (38 *brings the food and holds the bowl, feeding* 37 *from a spoon.*) It takes some time before a baby can hold a spoon for itself. Its hands have to learn how to grip and move the food to its mouth.

ARTIST. Just because our hands learn to do something, doesn't mean they'll always be able to do it. Look at this old woman.

39 can't bend her fingers. She tries to grip a knife and fork. She can only hold them clumsily and tries to cut some meat.

ARTIST. She has arthritis which makes her hands stiff. Holding things becomes difficult and painful.

GIRL. So we shouldn't take our hands for granted.

BOY. We might be unlucky and have something go wrong with them.

HANDSOME (*to* ARTIST). I think they're starting to understand how important hands are.

ARTIST. Yes. Thanks to you, Handsome, and my other Handy Helpers. (*Looks at watch.*) I must be going.

She packs away her things.

GIRL. I can't understand why there aren't more handscape artists around. There must be hundreds of other things hands are needed for.

HANDSOME. There are.

ARTIST. Perhaps you can think of some later, but I must be off to start my next handscape. The next one I shall not enjoy.

BOY. Why? What is it?

ARTIST. People, like the old lady, who are not so fortunate; those who, for one reason or another, have lost the use of their hands.

Picks up easel and box and walks off.

GIRL. I can't imagine having to manage without hands.

BOY. It would make everything much more difficult and some things impossible.

HANDSOME. But some people have to manage, no matter how hard life becomes for them.

HANDY HELPERS *stand.*

HANDY HELPERS. Whether handicapped by illness
Or accidents unplanned,
Some people have a life to lead
Without the use of hands.

A HANDY HELPER (*steps forward*).
I used to be a jockey.
Over sticks I'd win hands down;
That is, until last season,
When the last fence brought me down.
My mount fell squarely on me.

The surgeons tried to ease the pains, (*looks at hands*)
But I can't ride now – the movement's gone.
I couldn't hold the reins.

HANDY HELPERS. Whether handicapped by illness
Or accidents unplanned,
Some people have a life to lead
Without the use of hands.

ANOTHER HANDY HELPER (*steps forward*).
I was a shorthand typist,
Efficient, quick and neat,
On hand to help the bosses
With a deadline to meet.
But then I caught a virus.
It made my writing slow.
The bosses called a meeting.
A show of hands said I must go.

HANDY HELPERS. Whether handicapped by illness
Or accidents unplanned,
Some people have a life to lead
Without the use of hands.

ANOTHER HANDY HELPER *steps forward*.

HANDY HELPER (*quite cheerfully*). For years I was a policeman,
An old hand, I suppose you'd say,
Catching crooks red-handed, (*mimes nabbing someone*)
Helping lost souls find their way. (*Points the way to go.*)
(*Bitterly*) And then I became a hero,
Rescued children from a fire.
My hands were burned. They said:
'Accept a golden handshake and retire'.

HANDSOME. There's a lesson in these stories
Which we hope you'll understand.

GIRL. Don't take hands for granted.

BOY. If you've got them,

GIRL AND BOY. Lend a hand!

HANDSOME. Make your hands Handy Helpers.
   You've seen the sort of thing we mean.

ALL. Let others see at first hand
   Where *your* handiwork has been!

THE END

FURTHER SUGGESTIONS

We have seen, in this play, the many things that hands can do. Of course, there are many more. You can add further scenes to the play or find other ways of showing each other the 'handy' activities you have thought of – mime (which can become a guessing game), drawing and painting, or simply describing in words (with your hands firmly behind your back).

There are some things for which we use our hands which need the help of someone else. Try out some handscapes in pairs or groups.

Think of expressions which we use everyday involving 'hands'. We talk about 'going hand-in-hand', 'I've got to hand it to you', and 'hands up!'. Make a list of these expressions. What do they mean and why does the word 'hand' crop up in them so often?

Are there are other 'scapes' that you could make up? The senses – hearing, seeing, tasting, smelling, touching – might be good places to begin.

The play ends by talking about people who have no hands or are unable to use them properly. Why is this? Perhaps it would make a good piece for assembly and you can use the idea of the play for assemblies about the other themes too.

Marian and the Witches' Charm

David Wood and Dave & Toni Arthur

Introductory note

This play aims to be as flexible as possible. It can be performed in any space, with little or no special costume and scenery, and the minimum of props.

The cast can be virtually as large or as small as required. The whole cast is really a *crowd* of actors who *tell* as well as *react to* the story.

There is one song, sung at the beginning and at the end. Music for this is provided. But it is not essential that the song be *sung*; it can be simply chanted in rhythm – and in any event should be accompanied by percussion such as drum beats and tambourines.

A broad style of acting should be encouraged, in the manner of open-air strolling players, sharing their tale with the audience. Audience participation – booing, cheering, etc – is not essential, but would enhance the atmosphere.

The full-length musical play ROBIN HOOD is published by Samuel French Ltd.

Characters

All the actors, except perhaps THE SHERIFF'S WIFE, are part of the CROWD of folk celebrating May Day. They both narrate the story, (*in unison or with lines split up, as required*) and take part in it, becoming characters, setting the scene, becoming trees, and sometimes reacting to the story.

Individual Speaking Roles

THE SHERIFF'S WIFE
VOICE-IN-THE-CROWD 1
VOICE-IN-THE-CROWD 2
VOICE-IN-THE-CROWD 3
TRADER 1
TRADER 2
TRADER 3
THE BUTCHER'S WIFE
ALICE-A-DALE, MAID TO THE SHERIFF'S WIFE
MARIAN
VOICE-IN-THE-CROWD 4
VOICE-IN-THE-CROWD 5
WITCH 1
WITCH 2
WITCH 3
MAID
VOICE-IN-THE-CROWD 6
VOICE-IN-THE-CROWD 7

Individual Non-Speaking Roles

MARIAN'S ATTENDANTS
CASTLE GUARDS

STAGING THE PLAY

No scenery is necessary. The play flows swiftly from scene to scene, and each location is created by the actors. Certain props *are* necessary.

MARKET PLACE. A couple of pedlars' trays.
Some market stalls (*not* essential, although something to establish the BUTCHER'S WIFE would be a good idea).

ROOM IN THE CASTLE. A stool (optional) for the SHERIFF'S WIFE
A hand mirror
A bowl
A pig's head (a mask, to be secreted in the bowl)

MARKET PLACE. A set of stocks (even this *could* be mimed)

FOREST. Trees are 'played' by actors
Witches' cauldron (optional – it is never 'used')
Silver chalice
Green hood (big enough to cover the SHERIFF'S WIFE'S head, wearing her pig's head mask)

CASTLE. A mask (for MARIAN) of old crone

ROOM IN THE CASTLE. The hand mirror, as before

MARKET PLACE. Small purse of silver coins

Optional

If the play is to be performed in an open space, the actors 'arrive' singing, accompanying themselves on drum, tambourine, recorders, etc, encouraging the audience to clap in time with the music.

ALL. Dance, dance, dance all day,
    Dance your cares away,
    Pay the piper to play the tune,
    And dance with me today.

    (repeat if necessary)

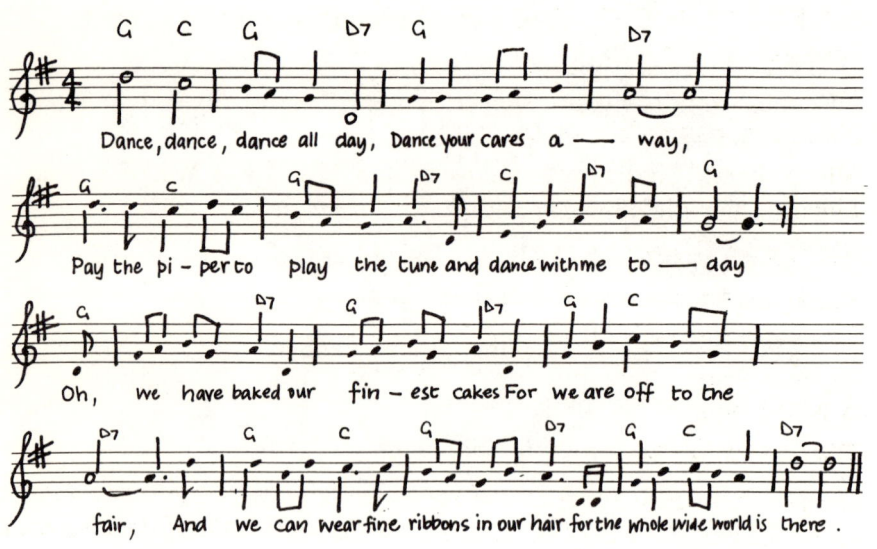

©Dave & Toni Arthur and David Wood

Fanfare – a blast on a hunting horn.

ALL. Marian and the Witches' Charm.

The actors need never leave the acting area. They can sit or stand behind the action or join the audience to watch, and sometimes comment, perhaps encouraging the audience to participate vocally.

The 'chorus' sections can be in unison or split up, as required. It may work best for some actors to be 'chorus' and some to be 'crowd', but sometimes they will merge together as one.

CHORUS (*to the audience*). Near Nottingham town in the merry greenwood
Lived a band of men led by young Robin Hood.
They robbed the rich and gave back to the poor
The money the Sheriff had taken by law.

The CROWD hiss.

The day you have joined is the first of May,
It's time for fun – it's a holiday,
And what makes the day a little bit better?
The Sheriff has gone to the King with a letter.

The CROWD cheer.

Robin has followed with his merry band
To take the gold from the Sheriff's hand.
So the villagers now may laugh and sing
A joyful song to welcome Spring!

The CROWD cheer.

Drum beat as all join hands and start singing or chanting, while dancing round in circles. Some of the circles could be inside others, dancing round in the opposite direction. But there is no need for formality. The dance should be rumbustious and spontaneous.

ALL. Dance, dance, dance all day,
Dance your cares away,
Pay the piper to play the tune,
And dance with me today.

Oh, we have baked our finest cakes
For we are off to the fair,
And we can wear fine ribbons in our hair
For the whole wide world is there.

Dance, dance, dance all day,
Dance your cares away . . .

Suddenly the singing and dancing is interrupted by the SHERIFF'S WIFE, *who has entered and angrily watched the celebration.*

SHERIFF'S WIFE. Quiet!

ALL (*with a gasp, some telling the audience*). The Sheriff's wife!

SHERIFF'S WIFE. Stop this unruly revelling! Just because my husband's away, there is no cause for celebration.

VOICE-IN-THE-CROWD 1 (*to the audience*). That's what *she* thinks!

Laughter.

SHERIFF'S WIFE. Silence! Or I'll see you suffer. Back to your work.

Disgruntled rumble.

VOICE-IN-THE-CROWD 2. But it's May Day.

VOICE-IN-THE-CROWD 3. A public holiday.

SHERIFF'S WIFE. The holiday is cancelled. By my orders. To work!

Boos.

The CROWD *reluctantly disperses to become a market scene. Traders and shoppers. Grudging market cries accompanying the change of scene.*

TRADER 1. Fresh milk. Straight from the cow!

TRADER 2. Ribbons and pins! Ribbons and pins!

TRADER 3. Gingerbread!

The cries can now mingle, eventually joined by:

BUTCHER'S WIFE. Lamb chops! Venison! Best pork!

The last phrase – 'best pork' – should be isolated, and the cue for the market scene to 'freeze' temporarily.

The SHERIFF'S WIFE *reaches the* BUTCHER'S WIFE.

SHERIFF'S WIFE. I'd like to see a pig.

BUTCHER'S WIFE. Then take a look in a mirror!

Laughter. The market scene unfreezes, and watches the following.

SHERIFF'S WIFE. None of your cheek. Deliver a pig to the castle tomorrow. It's for my birthday banquet.

BUTCHER'S WIFE. That'll be two silver pieces.

SHERIFF'S WIFE. Two silver pieces? I think not. You can give me the pig as a birthday present.

BUTCHER'S WIFE (*imitating the* SHERIFF'S WIFE). I think not.

SHERIFF'S WIFE. Unless you wish to be locked up in a dark dungeon full of poisonous snakes and a starving vulture!

The CROWD *boos.*

Ha, ha, ha. (*She starts to exit, singing*)

Happy birthday to me, happy birthday to me . . .

BUTCHER'S WIFE (*strongly*). I'll make her pay, you'll see . . .

SHERIFF'S WIFE (*as she exits*). . . . Happy birthday to me-ee . . .

As she goes, the CROWD *closes round and faces out to the audience.*

CHORUS. The Sheriff's wife, proud of her bargain so cheap,
Returned to the castle for her beauty sleep.
She paid no heed to the Butcher's wife's warning,
And woke fully rested for her birthday morning.

The CROWD *separates to reveal the next scene. It is the following morning. A room in the castle.*

The SHERIFF'S WIFE *is looking in a hand mirror, preening herself. Maybe she sits on a stool.*

SHERIFF'S WIFE. Mirror, mirror in my hand,
Who is the fairest in the land?
Who is this beauty that I see?
Goodness gracious, look – it's me!

CROWD. Ugh!

ALICE *enters with a bowl. She is humming happily.*

SHERIFF'S WIFE (*sharply*). Alice.

ALICE. Madam?

SHERIFF'S WIFE. Stop that dreadful noise.

ALICE. Yes, madam.

SHERIFF'S WIFE. How dare you hum.

ALICE. I was humming because I was happy, madam.

SHERIFF'S WIFE. Happy? How dare you be happy. (*To the audience:*)
Common serving girls are meant to work, not be happy.

The CROWD *hiss.*

ALICE. I am happy because it is your birthday, madam. Happy
birthday.

CROWD (*gently*). Aaaaah!

ALICE *gives the* SHERIFF'S WIFE *the bowl.*

SHERIFF'S WIFE. What's this?

ALICE. My present to you, madam. A bowl of morning dew. I gathered
it myself.

SHERIFF'S WIFE. Morning dew?

ALICE. 'Wash your face in the morning dew
And see a magic change in you.'

SHERIFF'S WIFE. Change?

ALICE. It's a saying. Ancient but true, my mother said. Morning dew
makes you fair.

SHERIFF'S WIFE. Meaning I'm ugly.

ALICE. No, no! But . . .

SHERIFF'S WIFE. Very well, I'll try it.

She washes.

ALICE and CROWD. 'Wash your face in the morning dew
And see a magic change in you.'

CROWD (*rising chant*). Change, change, change, change!

*The SHERIFF'S WIFE finishes washing. She looks up dramatically,
revealing that she now has a pig's face.*

SHERIFF'S WIFE. There. (*To the audience:*) How's that? Oink!

ALICE *screams. The* CROWD *laughs.*

(*The 'oinks' could be snorting noises.*)

What's the matter? Oink! Oink! (*Sensing something is wrong:*) What?
What? (*She looks in her hand-mirror. She screams.*) I'm a pig!

The CROWD *laughs.*

Oink! Witchcraft! I smell witchcraft! Oink! Alice, you wicked girl,
you've bewitched me! Oink.

ALICE. No! No, madam! Really!

SHERIFF'S WIFE (*realising*). Tonight's banquet! My guests! Oink. Me
a pig! Oink! I'll be a laughing stock! Oink! (*Grabs* ALICE.) Alice,
reverse this spell or you'll rot in hell! Change me back before the
banquet or be boiled in oil.

The CROWD *reacts with a gasp.*

ALICE. But I can't . . . I . . .

SHERIFF'S WIFE. Enough! Guards! Take her to the market place! Lock
her in the stocks!

Drum beats accompany the action as some of the CROWD *immediately
become GUARDS and swirl into action. They surround the screaming
ALICE, take her to the market place, and lock her in the stocks. Then
others mime throwing vegetables at her. ALICE mimes frightened reactions.
Laughter and enjoyment as the* CROWD *become an excited rabble. The
scene builds to pandemonium.*

This is interrupted by the arrival of MARIAN *and her attendants. She sees what is going on.*

MARIAN. Stop! Leave the girl alone.

The action freezes.

Some of the CROWD *'come to life' and face the audience.*

CHORUS. Would you believe, in the midst of this carry-on,
Who should arrive, but the fair Maid Marian?
What she saw made her face go pale,
For the stocks held the wife of young Alan-a-Dale.

The action unfreezes.

MARIAN. Shame on you. Release her.

VOICE-IN-THE-CROWD 4. Can't do that, lady.

VOICE-IN-THE-CROWD 5. Sheriff's wife's orders.

MARIAN. Cowards! Clear off, the lot of you!

The disgruntled CROWD *return to work. They mime market place activity as* MARIAN *rushes to* ALICE.

MARIAN. Alice . . .

ALICE. Marian, am I glad to see you!

MARIAN. What's happened?

ALICE. The Sheriff's wife says I'm a witch.

MARIAN. You a witch? That woman's a pig!

ALICE. You know?

MARIAN. Know what?

ALICE. She *is* a pig. Really. (*Whispers.*) She's got a pig's head.

MARIAN (*with a gasp*). She's been bewitched?

ALICE. Yes.

MARIAN. And she blames you?

ALICE. Yes. And if the spell's not reversed by tonight, I'm to die. Oh,

Marian, if only Robin were here . . .

MARIAN. Forget Robin. He's away on business! And anyway, Robin's not the only one with the bright ideas.

She starts to go.

ALICE. Where are you going?

MARIAN. Never you mind. Stay here till I get back.

ALICE (*in the stocks*). I don't have much choice!

MARIAN (*laughing*). Trust me!

She leaves.

During the following link, the CROWD become the trees in the forest. MARIAN makes her way through the trees, stooping to avoid branches, peering through the forest darkness. Her attendants follow.

Meanwhile, some of the CROWD turn towards the audience and become the chorus.

CHORUS. Maid Marian ran through the bramble and briar
To get help for poor Alice, now branded a liar.
To the heart of the forest she soon made her way
To the dark, leafy wildwood, where the weird witches stay.

The forest (CROWD) and CHORUS melt away as MARIAN and her attendants arrive at the WITCHES' home. At first they keep their distance from the three WITCHES who are at work round their cauldron.

WITCHES (*after a wild cackle*).
Bubble, bubble, at the double
We give help or we give trouble!
Spells for evil, spells for good,
By appointment to Robin Hood!

MARIAN approaches.

MARIAN. Witches!

WITCH 1. Who's there?

WITCH 2. 'Tis Marian.

WITCH 3. Welcome, my dear.

ALL THREE. Who can we do for you?

All cackle.

MARIAN. I need help, please, witches. A dear friend is in mortal danger.

WITCH 1. Not your Robin?

MARIAN. No, no. Alice-a-dale. She works in the castle. For the Sheriff's wife. This morning she was bewitched.

WITCH 2 (*concerned*). Alice?

MARIAN. No. The Sheriff's wife.

All cackle.

WITCH 3. It worked, sisters. It worked!

MARIAN. You know about it?

WITCH 1. Of course.

WITCH 2. Listen, dear Marian . . .

The WITCHES *circle round* MARIAN *in an anti-clockwise direction, chanting . . .*

WITCHES. We'll tell you all,
We'll show you all.
Just look in yonder glade
And there you'll see before your eyes
The trick that we have played.

The WITCHES *face the glade and point in a magical gesture.*

See!

As if by magic, members of the CROWD *act out the following witches' tale in the 'glade' area, watched by* MARIAN *and her attendants. Some of the* CROWD *become trees. The* BUTCHER'S WIFE *is seen coming through the wood.*

WITCHES (*in unison, or split up as required*).
The Butcher's wife came yesterday

To ask our help a debt to pay.

BUTCHER'S WIFE. Revenge, revenge!

WITCHES. She cried,

BUTCHER'S WIFE. I'll get her!

The BUTCHER'S WIFE *crosses to the witches' area.*

WITCHES. She told us of her planned vendetta.

BUTCHER'S WIFE. I want to buy a charm,

WITCHES. she cries.

BUTCHER'S WIFE. The Sheriff's wife I must surprise!

WITCHES. We offered her a pigs-head spell –

BUTCHER'S WIFE. The very thing!

WITCHES. She paid us well!

The BUTCHER'S WIFE *and* ALICE *mime the next part. The* CROWD
are still trees.

As daylight dawned she followed Alice,
Who gathered the dew in a silver chalice.

ALICE *collects the dew, putting it in a chalice, which she leaves on the
ground.*

When Alice turned her back a minute
She poured the magic potion in it.

The BUTCHER'S WIFE *pours the potion into the chalice, and hides.*
ALICE *takes the chalice and freezes.*

And this is why the Sheriff's wife
Will wear a pig's head all her life!

WITCHES *oink, then cackle manically.*

The CROWD, *the* BUTCHER'S WIFE *and* ALICE *disperse, leaving*
MARIAN *and her attendants with the* WITCHES.

MARIAN. No, no! You must give me an antidote to reverse the spell!

WITCHES. Impossible.

MARIAN. Alice's life depends on it.

WITCHES. Well . . .

MARIAN. Please, witches. In the name of Robin Hood!

WITCHES. We agree! Listen.
(*Giving* MARIAN *a green hood*).
First put her head in this green hood;
Green is the colour of the Lord of the Wood.
She must turn round thrice, touch her left toe,
Shout, "Pig be gone!" and the head will go.

MARIAN. Thank you, witches!

As the CHORUS *speak the following narrative, the* CROWD *act it out in mime.*

MARIAN *puts on a mask; the* SHERIFF'S WIFE *sits on a stool;* GUARDS *form a protective shield round her.*

There is a knockabout, funny, stylised fight sequence between the GUARDS *and* MARIAN *and her attendants. Percussion could echo the fight. The* CROWD *should encourage the audience to cheer each guard's defeat.*

CHORUS. She put on a mask to hide her fair face,
And gathered her friends to go to the place
Where the Sheriff's wife sat in her piggy-faced glory,
With guards all around her concealing her story.
They crept up behind them, without any sound,
Then pinched them, and tricked them and turned them around
Till they became dizzy, fell down on the floor,
Then Marian walked past them and knocked on the door.

MARIAN *mimes a door knock to a drum beat. The* SHERIFF'S WIFE *is the other side of the imaginary door.*

MARIAN (*calling, disguising her voice as a fortune teller*). Oh, wife of Nottingham's Sheriff!

SHERIFF'S WIFE. Oink!

MARIAN. I know you're in there.

SHERIFF'S WIFE. Go away. Oink! I'll see no-one.

MARIAN. You'll see me!

SHERIFF'S WIFE. Who is it? Oink!

MARIAN. A wise old woman of the wood. Here to help you.

SHERIFF'S WIFE. I don't need your help. Oink!

MARIAN. You do. (*Meaningfully:*) Don't be so pigheaded! Oink!
The SHERIFF'S WIFE *gasps and 'opens' the door, hiding her face in shame.*

SHERIFF'S WIFE. You know! Oink! My secret! Oink! How?

MARIAN. My eyes see through locked doors. They see through guilty hearts. The powers of my mind are only matched by the powers of my magic.

SHERIFF'S WIFE. Magic? Oink!

MARIAN. You have been bewitched. I can reverse the spell.

SHERIFF'S WIFE. Then, please, please do!

MARIAN. Listen and obey!

MARIAN *and the* SHERIFF'S WIFE *act out the spell, which is chanted by the* CHORUS. MARIAN *helps the* SHERIFF'S WIFE, *turning her, bending her, etc.*

CHORUS. First put her head in this green hood;
Green is the colour of the Lord of the Wood.
She must turn round thrice, touch her left toe,
Shout, 'Pig be gone!' and the head will go.

Drum plays a tense rhythm.

MARIAN. Go on, shout!

SHERIFF'S WIFE. I can't, I can't!

MARIAN. Shout, 'Pig be gone!', or pig you stay.

SHERIFF'S WIFE (*shouts*). Pig be gone!

MARIAN. Louder!

SHERIFF'S WIFE (*louder*). Pig be gone!

The drumming becomes faster and louder, building to a climax as MARIAN *pulls the hood off the head of the* SHERIFF'S WIFE, *revealing that the pig's head has disappeared.*

The CROWD *clap and call 'bravo'.*

The SHERIFF'S WIFE *looks in her hand-mirror to check all is well.*

SHERIFF'S WIFE. Thank you, thank you! How on earth can I repay you?

MARIAN. No need to pay,
Just heed what I say,
Remember, listen and learn:
Show *kindness* and *care*
Or else, I swear,
The Pig's Head will return!

SHERIFF'S WIFE. I will, I will! Kindness and care! I promise!

MARIAN. Farewell.

She exits.

SHERIFF'S WIFE. I must ready myself for my birthday banquet. (*Calls:*) Alice! (*Pause.*) Alice! (*Beginning to get cross.*) Where *is* the girl?

Enter a maid.

Where's Alice?

MAID. Why, in the stocks, madam.

SHERIFF'S WIFE. In the stocks? (*remembering*). Oh yes . . . .

She quickly looks in the hand mirror to check that her face is still normal.
Meanwhile . . .

CHORUS (*a whispered chant*). Kindness and care.
Kindness and care.

SHERIFF'S WIFE. Poor child. What villain could put Alice in the stocks?

MAID. But, madam, it was y. . .

SHERIFF'S WIFE. Order her release immediately!

MAID (*delighted*). Yes, madam!

She runs out.

VOICE-IN-THE-CROWD 6. Alice is free!

VOICE-IN-THE-CROWD 7. Alice is free!

The CROWD *cheer. The* SHERIFF'S WIFE *reacts, irritated by the noise.*
The cheering CROWD *happily takes over the acting area, some of them shouldering the freed* ALICE. *The* SHERIFF'S WIFE *storms through, as she did near the beginning of the play. She takes her mirror with her.*

SHERIFF'S WIFE. Quiet! Stop this unruly revelling. Just because my husband's away, there is no cause for celebration . . .

She stops to think, checking in the hand-mirror to see her face is still all right.
Meanwhile . . .

CHORUS (*a whispered chant*). Kindness and care.
Kindness and care.

SHERIFF'S WIFE. . . . but on my birthday there is *every* cause for celebration. Let today be a public holiday. And tomorrow!

The CROWD *cheer, then start singing and dancing. Drums, tambourines etc play.*

ALL. Dance, dance, dance all day,
Dance your cares away,
Pay the piper to play the tune,
And dance with me today.

During the song and dance, the SHERIFF'S WIFE *dances with abandon, but suddenly she bumps into the* BUTCHER'S WIFE.

SHERIFF'S WIFE (*angrily*). Aaaah!

BUTCHER'S WIFE (*before seeing it is the* SHERIFF'S WIFE). Oo, sorry.

SHERIFF'S WIFE. Clumsy oaf, how d. . . .

The CROWD *has stopped to listen. The* SHERIFF'S WIFE *stops. She looks in the hand-mirror to check that the pig's head has not returned. Meanwhile . . .*

CHORUS (*a whispered chant*). Kindness and care.

Kindness and care.

The SHERIFF'S WIFE *changes her intended* 'How dare you', *to:*

SHERIFF'S WIFE. How delightful to see you, dear Butcher's wife. Please forgive me. In my excitement yesterday – thinking of my birthday, selfish old me – I went off without paying you. Please accept my apologies and ten pieces of silver.

She hands the BUTCHER'S WIFE *a purse.*

BUTCHER'S WIFE (*amazed*). But it were only two.

SHERIFF'S WIFE. Take ten for your trouble. (*To the* CROWD.) Now everyone, dance, sing! Make merry!

The CROWD *cheers.*

Drums beat. The dancing and singing resumes.

The SHERIFF'S WIFE *regularly checks in her hand-mirror.*

MARIAN *enters, without her mask, and triumphantly greets* ALICE.

The CROWD *could encourage the audience to join in the dance.*

ALL. Dance, dance, dance all day,
Dance your cares away,
Pay the piper to play the tune,
And dance with me today.

We'll find fresh flowers to decorate the bowers
For we are off to the fair.
And we'll take a pail of the finest ale
For the whole wide world is there.

Dance, dance, dance all day,
Dance your cares away,
Pay the piper to play the tune,
And dance with me today.

_____

OPTIONAL

An extra chorus, during which the Actors could dance from the acting area.

Dance, dance, dance all day,
Dance your cares away,
Pay the piper to play the tune,
And dance with me today.

_____

THE END

FURTHER SUGGESTIONS

Some ideas to develop from this play have already been suggested following *Robin Hood and Friar Tuck*. This play has one interesting difference, however: it isn't the men who have all the fun and the adventures for once! Think of other popular stories and decide what adventures the less important characters might have.

Many stories have the same kinds of characters who are always expected to behave in the same way. Princes have to be charming, princesses are beautiful with long fair hair, witches and wizards must be wicked, and as for giants and dragons . . . Think of ways in which you *expect* other traditional story-characters to behave. Then think of ways they might turn out to be quite different and make up some plays or stories about *them*.